Them Times

To Linda & Leigh
Hope you enjoy it
Minnie & Syd — July 1997

Them Times

David Weale

Institute of Island Studies
Charlottetown
1992

Sixth Printing: July 1996

Series Editor: Harry Baglole
Editor: Laurie Brinklow
Illustrative Motif: P. John Burden
Layout/Design: Ken Shelton
Printing: Williams & Crue Ltd.,
Summerside, Prince Edward Island

Cover photograph courtesy Paul MacDonald.
Published with the kind assistance of the
Prince Edward Island Council of the Arts.

Canadian Cataloguing in Publication Data
Weale, David, 1942-
Them Times
(Island studies series; no. 4)
ISBN 0-919013-15-5

1. Prince Edward Island—Social life and customs.
2. Prince Edward Island—History—20th
century. * I. University of Prince Edward Island.
Institute of Island Studies. II. Title.
III. Series.

FC2618.W42 1992   971.7'03   C92-098604-8
F1047.W42 1992

Dedicated to the storytellers of the Island...

Acknowledgements

In writing this book I have gathered the voices of many Islanders. Without their stories and reminiscences, most of the chapters could not have been written. I only hope the pleasure of the reader will approximate the enjoyment I experienced in gathering the material during innumerable conversations with Islanders across the province over the past fifteen years.

I am also grateful to the many students who assisted me by interviewing family members, neighbours, and other elderly acquaintances in preparation for their written assignments in my classes at the University of Prince Edward Island. There are too many of them to identify individually, but I want to acknowledge that collectively they have made a major contribution to this volume. Often, in those classes, it was I who was the student.

A storyteller requires a good listener, and I would like to thank Wayne Collins, the attentive and genial host of "Them Times" on CBC Radio Charlottetown's "Island Morning," for being just that. Together we put to air more than a hundred programs and, remarkably, he never seemed to tire of the conversation. It made my role a most pleasant one.

I would also like to thank my editor, Laurie Brinklow, at the Institute of Island Studies, who skilfully guided the process of selection and renovation with a firm but considerate hand; and Harry Baglole, long-time friend and comrade, who has been active behind the scenes in the promotion of so many ventures which celebrate the history and society of this province—including this one.

Finally, and most especially, I would like to thank Evelyn McMurrer for her unfailing patience in translating my written and rewritten scrawl into readable type. For the one-hundred-and-one times I heard her say, "No problem," I now want to say, "Thanks, Ev."

D.W.
April, 1992

Island Studies Series

Within living memory a revolution has occurred in the green and gentle countryside of Prince Edward Island. Over the past few decades the changes have been so profound that the recent past is now referred to by many as "them times."

Based on the popular local CBC Radio series of the same name, *Them Times* is a collection of historical vignettes depicting Prince Edward Island before and after what some folklorists call "the break," that post-World War II period when the twentieth century seemed to hit the Island all at once. David Weale combines anecdotal reminiscences of Islanders with some of his own musings and observations of a way of life that has all but disappeared.

Them Times is the fourth in a series of occasional publications to be produced by the Institute of Island Studies. The previous titles are *A Stream Out of Lebanon* by David Weale, *The Bonshaw Hills* by Ian MacQuarrie, and *Black Islanders: Prince Edward Island's Historical Black Community* by Jim Hornby. The objective of the series is to publish, for both a popular and academic audience, short monographs dealing with aspects of the culture and environment of Prince Edward Island.

The Institute of Island Studies is a research, education, and public policy institute based at the University of Prince Edward Island.

Publishing Committee
Institute of Island Studies

Edward MacDonald, Chair   Allan Hammond
John Cousins   Michael Hennessey
John Crossley   Deirdre Kessler
Lawson Drake   Ian MacQuarrie

Contents

1 Introduction: Surviving "The Break"

5 The Other Side

8 Everybody's Business

11 Barefoot

14 In Bed With a Brick

17 Making it to the Grass

20 Spring Cleaning

22 Homemade Bread

24 Molasses

27 The Christmas Orange

29 Picking Potatoes

32 The Death Ship

34 Superstition

36 The Black Devil

39 Moonblindness

41 A Rooster's Worth

44 Count 'em, Belle

47 The Great Taboo

51 The Mixed Marriage

54 Remembering the Sabbath

57 Big Feelin'

61 Happy as a Clam

63 The Party Line

65 Leapo

68 Waste Not, Want Not

73 Soil Sacrament

75 God's Own Beast

79 An Awful Man to Work

83 Stuck Home

86 Islanders and Hippies

89 Well I Mind the Time....

92 Who Is an Islander?

95 Kitchen Table Surgery
97 Missing Fingers
99 The Forge
101 A Cake for the Wake
105 The Christmas Concert
107 Suppertime
108 The Change That Has Come Over God
110 Marooned in the Present
112 Island Zen

115 Them Times

INTRODUCTION
Surviving "The Break"

W hen we arrived on Prince Edward Island in 1948, the old
order of rural life was still more or less intact. For my parents, my sister, and myself, it was unlike anything we had
ever experienced. Our move from Calgary hadn't entailed leaving
the country, yet it seemed like emigration to a strange new world; or,
more accurately, like emigration to a strange old world.

I was only five but remember clearly the wet November day we
laboured up the clay road in our green, 1936 Dodge and pulled into
the manse yard. Today, forty-three years later, we are all still here. A
sister born in Alberton and a brother born in Summerside now live
in Ontario, but return annually to their "home" province. The
Weales are Islanders now, but the Island has changed drastically, and
the rural culture of our first encounter is largely a culture of memory.
How unlikely it would have seemed that the excited, wide-eyed,
small boy in the back seat would one day be sitting down, pen in
hand, to reflect affectionately on the disappeared way of life of his
Island childhood. Unlikely, indeed, but I begin.

My memories of that time are vivid. How well I recall the narrow, meandering clay road which brought us to that place. It reminds
me today of William Blake's aphorism, "Progress makes straight
roads, but the crooked roads, without improvement, are the roads of
genius." In winters the road all but disappeared and the sleighs
made their way as best they could, taking the path of least resistance
through the fields. For weeks in the spring that same road was almost
impassable—a veritable bog. Gradually it dried, and soon there were
clouds of red dust rolling into the fields on the hot summer wind. I
also remember that when you walked along our road at night, the
countryside was shrouded in a mysterious pre-electric darkness.

I recall the neighbours' farmyards, each with its sundry, shin-
gled assortment of barns, sheds, and outbuildings; stately orchards;
derelict fox-pens, overgrown and newly obsolete behind the barns;
cream cans sunk in the brook in a wooden box; separator parts hung
out to dry in the antiseptic sun; the pungent smell of potatoes and
turnips coming up through sloping cellar hatches; great square

1

kitchen tables; narrow, confidential back stairs; sedate pump organs in shaded parlours; shadows from coal-oil lamps; boiled tea, succulent canned chicken, and wild strawberry preserve served up with cream in little bowls; and Saturday night baths in a galvanized tub by the stove with a blanket over two chairs to block the drafts.

I remember, as well, the sounds of that time. Indoors, the thick bubble of porridge at a boil, and the aromatic sizzle of supper pork; the double bang of the back-door screen, and the blue-buzzing of September flies; the pendulous ticking of the gingerbread clock, and the gentle, purling whisper of the afternoon kettle. And, outdoors, the great hissing bluff of the territorial gander, the muscled fart of a workhorse, and the quiet, walking warble of a self-absorbed hen; the muted rumble of dumped potatoes, and the fragrant swoosh of forked-down hay; the muttered male cursing at broken equipment, and the echo of childish obscenities shouted down a well; the menacing chatter of the hay mower, and the tedious chewing of the cross-cut saw.

Then, at the end of the day, the ebbing cadence of evening conversation, and a final punctuating puff over the lamp's chimney.

I was too young at the time to reflect on the nature of the society I had entered, but thinking back I now understand that it was, at its heart, an ancient and bequeathed order, filled with manifestations of a folk tradition stretching back into the distant European past; a mutated old-country society which still operated according to many of the customs and manners that had crossed the ocean with the pioneers. I remember men like Charlie Rayner, and couples like Wallace and Linnie who lived across the road, and Charlie's brother George, and Billy and his sister, both unmarried, who lived out by the shore in Kildare. The cut and lilt of their language, the stories and sayings and superstitions which tumbled out of them so easily, the way they were around horses and other animals, their unhurried manual competence, their natural reserve, their patient resignation to tiresome and repetitive labour, and their general acceptance of the way of things were just some of the qualities they had inherited from their forebears—qualities which, in 1948, were still esteemed and useful. But not for long.

There were few at the time who recognized it, but we were living in a period of rapid cultural disintegration. Traditions and assumptions which had survived for centuries were in process of being displaced. That old rural society was coming apart at the seams and

3

I have always considered it my very good fortune to have arrived just before its demise. Like other Islanders my age or older, I have had the unique historical privilege of living on both sides of what some folklorists call "the break." It has been an experience both bewildering and exciting. One elderly Islander put it like this: "From 1945 everything changed. Nothing ever changed before that. It was the same lifestyle for two hundred years." He was not far wrong.

This book is, first of all, for the enjoyment of those many Islanders whose lives have overlapped this great change, or "break," in our provincial way of life; those who grew up in a period they now refer to as "them times." Doubtless most of them believed they would die in the same community, perhaps even in the same house, in which they were born. But since the days of their childhood, a very great disruption has occurred. In reading this book they will be reminded that they have lived in two epochs, and that they are a generation which arguably has witnessed more profound change in its lifetime than any other that has ever lived.

The book is also for the young people of the province: those who can scarcely imagine how their parents and grandparents once lived. It is for children like my two youngest sons who listen bemusedly to stories of their father's boyhood as though they were coming from ancient history. I hope this book will help bridge that gap for young Islanders by providing some insight into the rural society which nurtured and shaped their ancestors. Today, when I go back to Greenmount to show my children where I lived when I was their age, the community is almost unrecognizable. They see little there of what was, and it is that way all across the Island. While these brief essays cannot recapture everything that has disappeared, they can at least provide the young with some glimpses of that time and some small sense of continuity with what has gone before.

My purpose in writing is not to idealize "the good old days," for there was much about the period that was drab and difficult. The charm and poignancy of "them times" is not that it was altogether wonderful; rather, that it was altogether real and altogether ours.

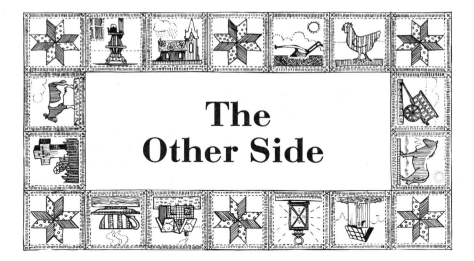

The Other Side

In many places a reference to "the other side" has definite metaphysical connotations. But not on Prince Edward Island. Here, "the other side" is a reference to the mainland. But, come to think of it, there is a similarity. For those Islanders who lived and died on this Island without ever setting foot on the mainland, "the other side" was, indeed, a mysterious, otherworldly domain, beyond the boundary of their geographically circumscribed lives.

George Brown, from Upper Canada, was one of the Fathers of Confederation who attended the Charlottetown Conference in 1864. While here, he wrote a letter to his wife with his impressions of the Island, including comments about the Pope household where he was lodged. When he came to his description of Mrs. Pope he observed, with some astonishment, "She was born on the Island and has never moved out of it in all her life. Many people here are in the same position, but are, notwithstanding, amazingly civilized."

Brown, his condescension notwithstanding, was correct in his observation that there were, and still are, those living here who have never been off the Island. One woman from Murray River, describing a mutual acquaintance, told me that "the only time he was off the Island was when he was up a tree," and I detected in her tone of voice the same insinuated reproach. She, like Brown, seemed to think that a life lived entirely on one small Island was, by definition, a small life. I'm not sure I want to get into all that, but what I do know is that there have been many Islanders who have had no great inclination to get away. Some of them, indeed, regarded it as something of an accomplishment never to have left.

One of my students told me recently about an elderly man from Cape Traverse who announced that neither he nor his wife had ever been off the Island. "I went across on the ferry once," he added, "but never set foot on the other side." I might be reading into his comments but it sounds to me like he felt he had had a close call. I also like the story about the man from up west who was asked if he had ever been off the Island. "No," he replied, "but I was to Summerside once with two fellows who were going to Boston."

There were many islands within the Island, and for countless people living fifty or sixty years ago any excursion outside their home district was exceptional. In those insular, self-contained communities there simply were few reasons, or opportunities, to go away. A man from the Tignish area went one autumn down to Bedeque to work at the potato harvest. When he returned after several weeks he was asked by a neighbour how he got along. He reported that they had treated him very well, and that the food was good. "But," he concluded, "I don't think I'll ever leave the Island again."

I was also told by someone from up west that there were old-timers from that end of the province who made their first visit to Charlottetown in the early 1960s to hear Conservative Prime Minister John Diefenbaker. It leaves me wondering whether or not there might be some Liberals up there who are still waiting for a sufficiently compelling reason to visit the province's capital.

But the story I like best of all is the story of the old woman from the western end who lived all her years just a few miles from the railway tracks. She heard the whistle blow at the crossing every day of her life, but died without ever having seen a train. For that woman, and others like her, a journey to the mainland would have seemed like a trip overseas.

I recall with fondness an old gentleman from High Bank named Lem Giddings who died just a few years ago. He lived in that part of the Island which provides a truly panoramic view of the mainland, and spent his entire life in that shore community looking out over the water every day for more than eighty years. Lem never strayed far from home, and I was struck by the novelty of his expression when he told me once about his visit to "the hill country." I inquired about this hill country and discovered he was talking about Bonshaw.

Lem was also the unofficial local weather forecaster, with an uncanny ability to read the sky and the wind and, as he put it, the "tracks on the water." During one of our weather conversations he remarked that under certain conditions Nova Scotia would "loom up" so close that you would almost think you could jump across. But Lem never jumped across, or even sailed across. Once, fishing lobsters, he did get as far as Pictou Island, so I guess you could say that he got off, but not across. He died without ever having set foot on "the other side"– a pure Islander.

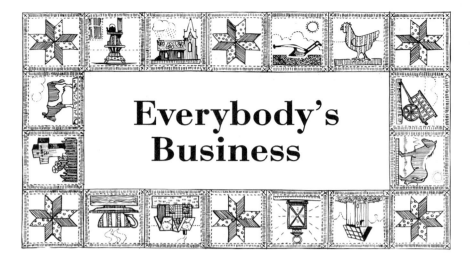

Everybody's Business

I recall the time an older woman was trying to identify a person I didn't know by referring to some of his relations. She became frustrated when I admitted I wasn't acquainted with any of the individuals she was mentioning. Finally, with just a touch of exasperation, she said, "It's awfully hard to tell a person about someone when they don't know people."

Not knowing people might have been my problem on that occasion, but it certainly wasn't a problem in those small, tightly knit communities of years ago, where everyone made it their business to know your business. As Father Francis Bolger once jokingly remarked to one of his classes at the University of Prince Edward Island, "It is the God-given right of every Islander to know the business of every other Islander."

Neighbours were a great blessing. People watched out for one another and shared with one another, and sometimes it was difficult to know where your own life ended and that of your neighbours began. There was a tremendous comfort in this, and a powerful sense of belonging, but it made privacy almost impossible. Your life could seem owned, and your actions perpetually monitored. If you went up the road instead of down, everyone knew, and wondered why. If you didn't go to Church on Sunday, or your wash wasn't on the line by nine, or you got a large parcel in the mail, or the doctor came by your house, or the minister, or there was a light in your window past ten o'clock, or your ring came over the telephone in the middle of the night– everyone knew, and wondered why.

Individuals were known and understood within the context of their families. There was a truth in that, but it could be discomfiting to realize that the community already had its mind made up about you from the time you were born. There was a tremendous expectation for you to be like your people, and how often I have heard an individual's behaviour explained summarily with the words, "Well, it's in that family you know," or, "His grandfather in his time was the very same."

Life under such circumstances could make you feel very hemmed in, very vulnerable, and sometimes very judged. It was like growing up in a straitjacket of community surveillance. Much of it was harmless, but the cumulative effect could be oppressive. There was no local law enforcement in those tight little districts, and no formal government. There didn't need to be. It was scrutiny which ruled your life, and the iron bars of custom and convention which kept you from getting out of line. It is entirely appropriate that the very first character introduced in the book, *Anne of Green Gables*, is Rachel Lynde who, in the words of L. M. Montgomery, "...was sitting at her window keeping a sharp eye on everything [and everyone] that passed."

Similarly, I can recall being in the kitchen of an elderly relation and hearing her wonder out loud as she stood in the window why Russell was going up the road at ten o'clock when usually he didn't go till near eleven. Nor would that be the end of it. I knew from experience that in all likelihood she would know the answer to her own question before the day was over. It's little wonder that many became tight-lipped and reserved, like Matthew in *Anne of Green Gables*, of whom it was said that he had never been known to volunteer information about anything in his entire life.

There were others who seemed rather to enjoy all the peeking and prying. I recall hearing the story of the man from Mount Albion who decided in his later years to move to town. He stayed one winter and then moved back out home. When someone asked him how he had liked it he replied, "Oh it was all right, and handy to get around, but the trouble with livin' in town is that nobody knows your business."

On any given day the neighbours would be liable to know who was setting bread, who was setting hens, who was setting their hair, and who was setting off for somewhere. One of the best stories I ever heard about the extent of this "neighbour-knowing" was related to me by Jim Craig who grew up in East Baltic. He said that if you were out in the yard in the wintertime and a sleigh went up the road, it wasn't necessary to lift your head in order to know who was going by. "You could tell by the sleigh-bells," he said.

"Did all the bells in the community have a different ring?" I asked, somewhat incredulously.

"Oh it wasn't just the sound," he explained, "it was more the rhythm. Every horse had its own particular gait and that made the bells ring differently." Amazing, I thought. The neighbours knew not only your peculiarities, but the peculiarities of your mare as well.

It could be confining and stultifying at times, all that communal togetherness – a heavy harness of opinion and expectation thrown over the vitality of individual inclination. And sometimes there must have been a very great temptation to climb up to the peak of the barn on a clear evening and shout aloud for all to hear, "Mind your own business!" But on balance I'm inclined to agree with Oscar Wilde who once noted that there is only one thing in the world worse than being talked about, and that's not being talked about.

Courtesy Mary Cairns

Barefoot

With what eager anticipation the children would wait for that certain spring day when they could kick off their gumboots, roll down their heavy woollen socks, and go forth into the world in that blissful condition known as barefoot. It was a great sensual pleasure to be roaming the world on naked soles with naked toes. One man said that you just can't get a feel for the earth in shoes the way you can in your bare feet. "It would be something like makin' love with a pair of mitts on," he mused philosophically.

If you ventured out barefoot too early, before the earth had warmed, you might end up with a bad case of chilblains. That, at least, was what your mother always said. It sounded serious, though I must confess that to this day I don't know what they are. But as far as most youngsters on the Island were concerned, it was the sooner barefoot the better. One woman who grew up in the Brae in the 1920s put it like this: "Almost as soon as the snow left we would kick off the shoes. I think the date we would go for was about May 24th. There would be a race to see who was the first one, and we would go that way late into the fall, sometimes until it snowed."

The tactile delights of going barefoot were many. Some people remember happily the feeling of the road sand, and, by mid-summer, the thick layer of dust which had accumulated in the low spots. It was fine and soft, like talcum powder, and splashed like warm water when you stepped in it. Then, when it rained, there was the cool mud which oozed and squished up exquisitely between your toes.

One woman from Kildare recalled fondly the feeling of the moss-covered logs which lay across the brook. She said the sensation was just "heavenly." There was also the pleasant feeling of the shiny, worn boards on the school floor, and the unaccountably delightful experience of running through a pasture and snapping off the heads of daisies or brown-eyed Susans between your toes.

My favourite mental picture of barefoot boys and girls is out of the memory of one woman who recalled dancing in the puddles. "We all used to go to school barefoot," she said, "and we would walk in the rain and dance in the puddles. It was such fun. You would get your arse-end all wet, but it didn't matter. It was worth it."

Memories of going barefoot are not all pleasant. One man spoke of the "stone bruises" he would have on his heels from coming down hard on undetected rocks. Thistles were another problem, and stubble – that was nasty. The sharp stalks of the cut grain brought pain to all but the most hardened soles, and most older people recall that it was best to run through the stubble. Walking gingerly only made it worse. But when your feet toughened up from weeks of going barefoot you could walk or run bravely over almost anything. "Your feet got so tough," said one man, "that you could run over a bunch of broken rocks, a load of gravel, or a field of stubble, and you'd think you were walkin' across the kitchen floor." Other hazards were the plops of hen and goose droppings in the yard, and the great wide cow-pies in the pasture. They caused no pain, but did detract somewhat from the aesthetics of the barefoot experience.

By the time the fall arrived and the weather turned cold, you would be glad to get back into a pair of shoes or boots. But sometimes there would be no money until after the potato harvest, which meant that some children had to pick potatoes in October in their bare feet. More than one person has told me that they can remember picking barefoot when there would be frost on the ground.

A man from Indian River recalled the unpleasantness of going for the cows in the fall. "Goin' for the cows in the mornin' in summer wasn't too bad," he said, "but when it got colder in the fall, that was something else." But he did find a way to make the task more bearable. "In mid-October," he explained, "I would run over to where a cow was lying down, kick her up to her feet, and then stand on the spot where she was lying to get my feet warm before the trip back."

Recently I was sitting with friends around the table after dinner when one of the young men in the group mentioned that he had just purchased a pair of Reebok pumps. An older woman asked him why in the world he would spend so much money for a pair of sneakers. "Are they really that much better?" she asked skeptically. "Oh I don't know," he replied, "but when you get them on and pump them up they just feel good on your feet. Maybe it's just in my mind, but I think they're worth it."

For older Islanders, going barefoot – just like Reebok pumps– was a state of mind. After all these years, the association with the coming of spring, the closing of school, and the carefree pleasures of long summer days bring a shudder of delight to old hearts, and a nostalgic wiggling of toes in corduroy slippers.

Courtesy Harold MacLeod

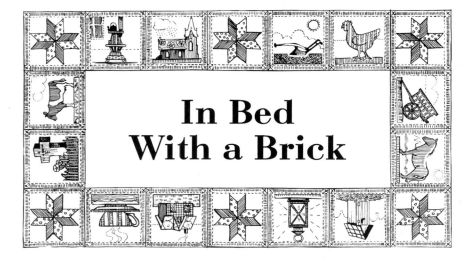

In Bed
With a Brick

When the long, corn-yellow days of Indian summer had disappeared and the wet, glowering days of gray November had arrived, the people of the Island got ready for winter, the way a city in wartime might prepare for a long seige. Like an invading, alien force, the pitiless cold encroached. This was one enemy you couldn't keep out of your community, or even out of your house. With diligent preparation and heroic effort you might drive him from your kitchen and keep him out of your bed, but that was as much as you could do. You just staked out a little territory and shivered through until spring.

In many of those old farm homes, the only warm place during most of the winter was the kitchen; or, more precisely, that part of the kitchen nearest the stove. One woman recalled that in her home, even with the kitchen fire burning, the potato skins or "jackets" on the kitchen table would sometimes be stiff with frost before the dinner meal was finished, and that you would wait forever for the cold molasses to make its glacial descent out of the jar onto your bread. Another person said that the frost on the inside of their kitchen windows would be just as thick as that outside. "As kids," she said, "we would take turns pressing our tongues on the window to make a spot to see if it was day or night."

Going to bed required a hero's heart. Armed with a hot brick in a sack, or a granite stone in a knitted cover, or a piece of hardwood, or a bag of salt or grain, or even the Eaton's catalogue warmed in the oven since suppertime, you screwed up your courage and headed upstairs to the bedroom. Apparently there were also some people who took the covers off the stove and wrapped them in layers of newspaper as a bed-warmer, and others who filled a stone mason jar with hot water. It was a great adventure and one man told me that "the only difference between the bedroom and outside was that it wasn't blowing quite so hard in the bedroom." Those old, poorly insulated homes were not very tight, and another survivor from that era said that when there was a storm it was so drafty, "You could clean grain on the back stairs."

I have a personal recollection of sleeping in an unfinished bedroom where the tips of all the nails from the shingles on the roof were visible. In the morning, after an especially cold night, there would be a small ball of white frost on the end of each of those nails. I also recall that when it stormed at night there would be a considerable drift of snow just inside the door on the kitchen floor. A man from Murray River shared a similar memory. "In the mornin'," he said, "the frost would just be glistenin' on the walls, and the kettle would be frozen on the stove. Under those conditions," he added, "it didn't take you long to get your gear on, I'll tell you that." Another older Islander who was a boy during the 1930s said that his mother, before retiring, would put things in the oven to keep them from freezing during the night and that often her efforts were not successful.

Another memory I have of those frigid bedrooms is of the frozen-over chamber pot under the bed. There was a curious sense of childish conquest in directing a stream of steaming urine at a single spot in the ice until it punched through. If you had anything left, you started over again at a new spot. This might or might not say anything important about my mental state at the time, but it does say a good deal about how cold it was in the house.

A friend who grew up in Albany said he remembers clearly the ritual of dressing and undressing under those Arctic conditions. He said that in winter he would always take off his clothes under the covers, and that in the morning he would reach out and pull the clothes into the bed so they would warm up just a little before he put them on for the day. I also like the vivid picture conjured up by a former schoolteacher. In one house where she stayed, her room was so cold that sometimes in the morning her hair would be matted thick with ice from the condensation of her own breath.

They were difficult times, but there was something wonderfully simple and focused about life under those severe circumstances. Existence, after all, attains a very great clarity of purpose when you are trying to keep from freezing to death. I sometimes think that what was good about the good old days is that individuals were so busy trying to keep alive and warm that they never got around to asking all those bedeviling, existential questions which are the luxury of a pampered, thermostatically-regulated consciousness.

Making it to the Grass

There is no real springtime on the Island, just the long intermittent and grudging retreat of winter. Long-time residents have learned that a warm day in March or April is no reason to put away the boots or take off the snow tires. It's just a tease: something to get your hopes up before the next snowstorm. Yet many of us, perpetual optimists, fall for it year after year.

In many places, winter means snow, and spring means rain. But not here. Not on the Island. In this province, winter most definitely means snow, but spring means sleet or drizzle, which, as I make it, is precipitation which can't make up its mind. On April 26th, 1887, Alexander Larkin of Cascumpec wrote in his daybook: "Very stormy. Thick sleet. Mostly snow. Blowing hard from the N.E." And that, I'm afraid, is what Islanders call spring.

Though its approach was hesitant and rather bad-natured, there were a few clear signs that spring had finally arrived, or at least that winter was almost over. When muscular rhubarb began shouldering up through the cold earth, and estuaries and brooks were suddenly black with smelt; when the triangles and trapezoids of harbour ice invited the quick feet of schoolboys, and fields broke through the snow cover in parallel lines of fall ploughing; when the itinerant sheep-shearer came by with his clippers, and the Micmac woman with her baskets and May flowers; when it was time for taking away the banking and opening the cellar hatch to the ventilating breeze;

when farmers and fishermen flexed and fisted their thick hands, impatient with winter waiting, and children began asking if it was time for bare feet; when it was time to take the storm windows off the house, and the old Ford or McLaughlin off the blocks; and when raucous geese announced from the sky the turning over of the season, the men and women of the Island roused themselves from their long winter's detention, happy to have survived for another season of greening and growth.

Winter was a season of grim endurance, and for many old people there was real concern about making it through until spring. They hung on and hung on, especially in March and April, waiting for the reinvigoration of warmer weather. It was the same in the barn. On many farms the cattle would be so weakened by the long winter's confinement, and so malnourished from want of good fodder, that some of them would go down and not be able to get back up on their feet. Some people called this condition "the lifters," presumably because the animals had to be hoisted to their feet in order to get them outside. One man, in recounting this for me, said the farmers would be greatly relieved when their animals would "make it to the grass."

Of all the images of spring, there is one which stands out most vividly in my mind. On a sunny morning just before Easter, a priest in his rectory was awakened by sounds coming from the direction of the church. He looked out the window and saw an old female parishioner, who had come early to the church for Mass, dancing in the morning light and watching her own shadow on the side of the church. It was spring, the sun was shining, and she was still alive. Her dance was a celebration, the ancient vernal dance of perennial awakening. Once more she had "made it to the grass."

19

Spring Cleaning

The task of spring house-cleaning weighed heavily on women's minds. Beginning mid-winter it was never far from their thoughts or tongues, and from the way they talked it was evident that spring cleaning was more than an anticipated chore. For many it was a compulsion. "There was a fall cleaning as well," recalled one woman, "but the spring cleaning, that was the big thing."

The compulsiveness had a great deal to do with the neighbours, and the unspoken yet palpable rivalry which existed between them. "Did you get to your spring cleaning yet?" might sound like a perfectly innocent inquiry, but in that society where indolence was a cardinal vice, it was a loaded question. One person told me that some women would be anxiously peeking out their windows at their neighbours' clotheslines to be sure they weren't being upstaged. Louis MacDonald from Cornwall recalled a woman from his area, a "fanatical housekeeper," who joined the Women's Institute but stopped going to meetings after a couple of years. When asked why she no longer attended, she replied with perfect candour, "I don't need to go anymore because I've already seen the inside of every house in the district."

There was also something else that drove them. There's little doubt in my mind that the throwing open of the windows, the sponging down of morescoed walls with warm water and ammonia, and the draping of quilts and curtains over pagewire fences had at least as much to do with the mental health of the farmwife as with the cleanliness of the house. This was soul work: a redemptive act of inner cleansing with rags, mops, and goose-wing dusters.

In those polished hardwood days, where the circumstances of a woman's life were so largely preordained, and where there was so little opportunity for replacing or even rearranging the old furniture of disappointment and regret, the ritual of spring cleaning was an important symbolic undertaking. It wasn't just the year's accumulation of dust and dirt that had to be dealt with, it was also the winter's accumulation of drudgery, repetition, and constraint that needed scouring and ventilating. That was the real grime. As one person expressed it, "Fussy! you never seen the like. If it didn't shine it wasn't clean. A woman's house was her person you see, and her pride and joy."

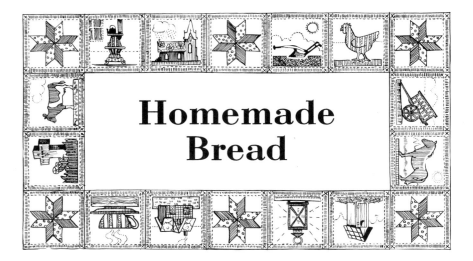

Homemade Bread

In the evening, just before bedtime, a batch of bread-dough was mixed with the yeasted sponge. It was placed in a large bowl or pan, covered with a cloth—or in winter a coat, or several coats—then placed in a warm spot near the stove. While the family slept, and the clock ticked, it rose.

I am aware that a lump of bread-dough on the rise is not very dramatic, but think of ten thousand lumps of dough, all rising simultaneously in ten thousand kitchens across the province. Now that is what I call a major event, a veritable uprising. All right, all right, so it's not very exiting. It's commonplace. Ordinary. I know that. But there is a kind of splendour and power in those ordinary things. The rolling over, punching down and rising up of the bread-dough— the mixing, kneading and setting—was just one of the daily tasks which gave definition and purpose to the lives of tens of thousands of Island farm women and their families. It was part of the deep, sustaining rhythm of work which moved an entire society.

I know a woman from a family of ten children who told me that for years her mother baked bread every single day, except Sunday. That day off meant, of course, extra baking on Saturday. She said her mother went through two hundred pounds of flour each month, and that the family consumed six very large loaves every day. Another elderly woman told me that a wise young man would choose a wife with one eye on the bread she made, for, if it wasn't good, you knew you would be eating it four times a day for the rest of your life.

Someone once told me a story about a family where the wife was a notoriously poor bread-maker. For years her husband endured in sullen silence the affliction of her bad baking, but one day could contain himself no longer. He began to complain. It was too dark, too heavy– and, once he started, the pent-up irritation began to mount in intensity. Finally, his offended wife cut him off. "You shouldn't be complainin'," she chided. "Don't you know this is the very bread Jesus gave the multitudes when he fed the five thousand." There was a brief pause, and then the husband replied, "Yes, I can believe it, and now I understand why there were twelve basketfuls left over."

I recall as a young man sitting in Celia Penny's kitchen in Beach Point watching her make bread at the table. Each movement of her hands and arms, each forward push of her body, each sprinkling of flour, each deft cutting of the lump, each rounding under of each loaf was performed with such grace and proficiency that it seemed to me more a ritual than a chore. No surpliced priest at his altar ever performed a more sacred task than that aproned woman at her kitchen table, for it was the stuff of life in her hands, and in her hands the answer to the prayer, "Give us this day our daily bread."

Molasses

I t wasn't exactly the food of the gods. Indeed, it might better be described as the food of the common folk, which is to say, the food of Prince Edward Islanders. In most rural homes there was no such thing as a meal without it. It was, of course, molasses—sticky ambrosia of the poor.

Simple fare it was, but sweet and thick, and dark with Caribbean sun, and if it hadn't been so inexpensive it might have been considered a very great delicacy, fit for a Queen's breakfast. But it was cheap. You could get a whole gallon for fifty cents, and some people bought it by the puncheon. It graced the tables of the lowly, providing an exotic contrast to the ordinary potato and oatmeal fare of country cuisine. In the minds of some people, molasses became forever identified with scarcity. One woman told me that when she had her teenage friends over for supper she would implore her father not to haul out the molasses jar for dessert. That was in the 1950s and, for her, molasses had become a sign of poverty and backwardness. Another woman, in her nineties, recalled a niece who went to a birthday party at the minister's house in the 1930s. When she got home she told her mother it was the queerest supper she had ever had. "There was," she reported indignantly, "no bread and molasses."

There were many meals that consisted of nothing more than bread and molasses and a cup of tea—a combination known in some quarters as "a poor man's meal." I have also heard of some especially destitute families where the molasses was watered down to make it go further. The person who told me this added with a wry smile,

"The only thing that wasn't watered down at our place was the water." When the cows went dry in the wintertime, molasses, blended with a little canned milk and some water, was sometimes used as a substitute. This sweet mixture was called "switchel," and in some homes it was the custom to dip each spoonful of oatmeal in the switchel jug before eating it.

Molasses was also routinely used as one of the ingredients in many of the home remedies concocted by farmwives for ailing family members. There was ginger and molasses for a hacking cough, alum and molasses for the cramps, soda and molasses—boiled until frothy—for a cold or sore throat, and sulphur and molasses, a most disagreeable mixture given to family members as a springtime tonic. Two teaspoons of sulphur were stirred into half a cup of molasses, producing a nauseating paste which seemed, in the minds of protesting children, a substance totally unfit for human consumption, something more suitable for lubricating machinery than for purifying the body. Many still gag just to think of it. "We would take so much of it," said one man, "that you could notice the sulphur in the clothing ... and when the clothes were hung over the stove to dry and the water would drop on the stove, you could see the blue sulphur flame."

Molasses also went to school with you. How well I remember those thick pieces of homemade bread, soaked through with molasses, wrapped up in a newspaper. One woman recalled a boy in her school who had a cotton schoolbag, and how, on a hot day, "the molasses from his sandwich would be dripping through onto the floor." Other students, with no taste for soggy bread, would take their molasses to school in a small jar and pour it over the bread when they were ready to eat. On many days those same students would have for their sweet—a molasses cookie.

Full-strength or diluted, as medicine or with meals, you couldn't get away from molasses. It was there in your beans, in your ginger cookies, in both the Christmas pudding and the sauce, in your taffy, even in your moonshine and spruce beer. You had it over bread, over bannock, over biscuits, over Johnnie cake, over your porridge, and, invariably, over your hands. When the Carnegie Libraries opened on Prince Edward Island—I believe it was in the 1930s—one librarian was very concerned about the condition of the books being returned from the rural homes. Many of them, she complained, were coming back with the pages stuck together with molasses.

In 1955 a girl from western Canada came to Prince Edward Island for nurses' training. She wrote back to her family in Manitoba about the different foods she had encountered. She mentioned, among other things, salt herring and beet-and-celery salads. Also, she observed with some revulsion, "They serve molasses with every meal. They eat it on bread!"

They certainly did. On bread, and on just about everything else.

The Christmas Orange

Perhaps the greatest difference between Christmas today and Christmas "them times" is that "them times," people were poor. Not that there aren't any poor today, but back then everyone was poor – or almost everyone. It wasn't a grinding, end-of-the-rope kind of poverty. Most everyone had food enough to eat and warm clothes to wear. The woodshed was filled with wood, the cellar with potatoes and carrots, and the pickle barrel with herring or pork. In many ways it was an era of plenty, so you might say that rural Islanders weren't poor, they just didn't have much money.

What strikes me forcibly when I speak to old people is that the scarcity of money made it possible to receive very great pleasure from simple, inexpensive things. I know, for example, that for many children an orange, a simple orange, was a Christmas miracle. It was the perfect golden ball of legend and fairy tale which appeared, as if by magic, on December 25th. In that drab world of gray and brown, it shone mightily like a small sun.

The orange was a kind of incarnation of Christmas itself, the very spirit and embodiment of the Christmas season. For many Islanders the most vivid, evocative memory of that blessed time is the memory of an orange in the toe of their stocking. One woman from a large family in Morell said that at her home you were fortunate if you received a whole orange for yourself. She recalled some lean years when she received half an orange, and was happy for it.

For children who ate oatmeal porridge for breakfast virtually every day of their lives, and had molasses on bread most days in their school lunch; for children who looked at fried potatoes almost every evening for supper and considered turnip scrapings a special evening snack; for these children an orange was a marvel, something almost too wonderful and prized to be eaten—an exotic, sensuous wonder.

One woman confessed that she kept her orange for a week after Christmas, kept it in a drawer. Several times a day she would go to her hiding place and take out the orange just to fondle it, and smell it, and to anticipate joyously the pleasure which was to come. Eventually it had to be eaten: deliberately, unhurriedly, ceremoniously, and gratefully. Piece by piece, and finally the peeling—it was all eaten, and it was all good.

But soon it was gone. All that remained was the hope that there would be another Christmas and, if God would be good, another orange.

David Weale collection

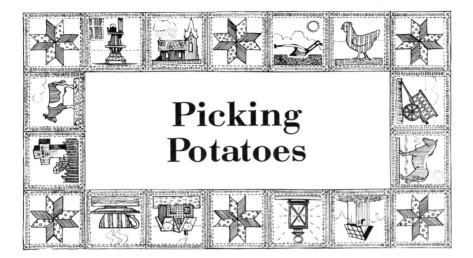

Picking Potatoes

They were long days, easily the longest of my life. I recall
hour after desolate hour on my knees, reaching for potatoes
which had been thrown this way and that by the digger,
then picking up the basket and dumping it in the bag, and then the
whole thing over again, and over again, and over again. It was torture,
and each day seemed an eon. I remember clearly that bright October
afternoon in a field in Sherbrooke when the sun stopped in the sky.
I was sure of it. Every time I checked it was in exactly the same place.
Finally I turned my face up and said out loud, "Get down will you.
Get down, damnit."

It was hard work for a kid, especially one who hadn't been
raised on a farm. I recall a skim of snow on the ground when we went
out one morning, and the uncomfortable feeling of cold, damp clay
packed up hard underneath all my fingernails. I also remember trip-
ping over the tangle of dead tops as I staggered to the nearest bran
bag with my heavy basket. There was the rough rub of coarse jute
against raw knuckles as I attempted to dump the heavy basket, and
frequent, tearful spilling and re-picking.

Everyone was assigned a stepped-off length of the drill. That
was your responsibility and the only way you could get a rest during
the entire day was if you managed to finish your section before the
man on the tractor turned over the next. I don't think that ever happened to me, and I can recall clearly my sullen, childish anger at him

for getting so far ahead. I also wondered, hatefully, why he, a strong man, should get to drive while I, a mere boy, was straining my guts trying to keep up with him. To look sideways and see three or four sections dug and waiting was enough to break your heart. I felt persecuted, and remember wishing with all my might that he would run out of gas, that a field stone would break the digger chain, that it would rain, or that the world would come to an end.

The high point of the day was dinner: roast beef (always slightly overcooked), rich dark gravy with plenty of floating onion, a mountain of mashed potatoes, turnips and carrots, homemade bread, a thick slice of pumpkin pie for dessert, and all the milk you could drink. It almost made the whole thing worthwhile. Almost.

At the end of the week I got paid. Ahh, those bills, some ones and twos, even some blue fives, and all for me! I shoved the money down deep in my pocket and exulted in the achievement it represented. I also recall flexing my biceps under my fall jacket and imagining they were much bigger and harder than those of most boys my age. There was a kind of aching satisfaction in that moment, and first faint stirrings of emergent manliness.

The Death Ship

Y ou must try to imagine the scene through the eyes of an impressionable twelve-year-old. It was late fall, and the trees were all ragged with last leaves. By the time you finished the barn work with your father there was just a patch of light in the west, fast closing to end the day. The world seemed unsettled somehow, and you knew it would probably rain and blow against the windows all through the night. It felt good to go inside.

There was company that night. Alex, a bachelor from just up the road, was sitting at the kitchen table and was already in the middle of the story about the time the ladder slipped when he and Martin were painting the church steeple, and how he got saved by the cross. You'd heard that story before but were happy to hear it again. That's how it was with Alex. Your father said he wasn't much good for anything else, but that his stories could make you forget all your troubles.

Later in the evening, soon after your mother had served the tea and the lunch plate, there would be ghost stories and fantastic tales of forerunners which had frequently been seen in the community. You knew if you were really quiet, and sat just outside the circle of lamplight, your mother might forget you were there, and you shivered with a kind of wonderful dread as you anticipated how frightened you would be when Alex would tell the story of the ghost at the little bridge, or of the time his father met a mysterious sad woman on the road who disappeared suddenly as she passed by, or about the coffin-maker in the village who always knew when he was about to receive an order because the saws hanging on the wall would begin to rattle unaccountably.

But of all Alex's stories, the one about the death ship was your favourite. It was about a man in the next community. In his dreams he would see a large masted vessel sail right up over the land and stop in front of a house. A person from the house would come out and board the ship, which would then sail away. Soon after the dream, the person who had boarded the ghostly vessel would die. Often the dream was about people who were ill, so the death was no great surprise. Sometimes, however, it was about young, healthy individuals, but invariably there would be a tragic accident, or a sudden illness, confirming once again the power of the vision.

One day the dreamer himself became ill and informed his family he would soon be gone. They attempted to reassure him, but he was adamant. "I have dreamed the dream of the ship," he explained.

"Oh, Father," they said, "you have had that dream many times before."

"Yes," he said, "but this time it was different. This time the ship sailed to our house, and it was myself who boarded."

The next day he was dead.

Superstition

It was at a small family gathering one Sunday. We were chatting over dessert when the woman sitting next to me remarked quietly, apparently to herself, "Mmm, there's a little money in there." I turned to look and discovered that she was peering into her teacup. It didn't surprise me much, as I had often seen her mother do the same thing. I looked closely, and, sure enough, there it was, a small island of foam and bubbles floating on the surface of her tea.

She didn't really believe it, nor did I. Not for a minute. At least I don't think we did. But isn't that just the power of superstition. You can protest your disbelief as much as you like, and cover yourself in the invincible garment of empirical objectivity, but you can never be entirely sure. There is always that tiny question mark at the back of the mind, the unspoken "what if?" After decades of scientific teaching in our schools and universities, many of us remain inveterately, enduringly, incurably superstitious. Beyond the realm of observable cause and effect, beyond the plane of measurement, in that deep place where mind and matter blend together unaccountably, the mystery remains.

Please don't get me wrong. I'm not making a case for superstition. I don't really believe that a double-yoked egg presages a marriage, that whistling aboard a boat will bring bad fortune, or that pissing on the side of the road will cause a sty in the eye. The latter, obviously, is just a scare tactic to help civilize little boys.

I don't believe that you can get rid of ugly warts by rubbing them with a piece of raw meat and then throwing it over your left shoulder into the raspberry patch, or by wishing them onto a corpse; or, that if you shudder inexplicably, it means that someone is walking over the site of your future grave. Nor do I believe that it's bad luck to place three lighted lamps on a table, to look at the new moon for the first time through glass, or to count the number of buggies or sleighs in a funeral procession. And what sane person could possibly believe that a broom falling across a door, or an extra place set at the table by accident would bring a visitor, or that if your door blew open it meant that someone was wishing to be with you? The credulity and wishful thinking in all of that is transparent.

And I certainly don't believe all that morbid foolishness about a bird in the house. One spring when a hapless starling came down the chimney, through the stove into the house, I did what anyone would do. I opened the door, got the broom, and chased the frightened creature outdoors where it belonged. And then I said confidently, "That's that." But there was a discomfiting little voice within me, perhaps the voice of some long ago Celtic ancestor, which echoed, "You hope that's that."

The
Black Devil

There is a dark side to human experience, a darkness in others and, what is even more fearsome, a darkness in ourselves. In our tradition the name for that menacing, malignant presence—that shadow across our souls—is Satan, or the Devil.

Years ago, before secularization and psychoanalysis, the Devil was no mere abstraction. He was a real presence in the midst of life, as real and omnipresent as God himself, and if God was to be praised, it was no less your duty to spurn the Devil. If you gave him an entrance, any small opening of idleness or spiritual inattentiveness, any tiny crack of willed misbehaviour, he would be sure to slip in and triumphantly claim your soul. "The Devil finds work for idle hands," was one way of expressing the danger. "Cut your fingernails on Sunday and the Devil will be after you all week," was another. And in some homes if you heard a knock on the door you would never shout, "Come in." It might be the Devil, and I have heard more than one story where horrible, cloven handprints were burned deeply into the wood of the door by the indignant, unwelcomed visitor.

In the stories which were told, this dark malefic spirit appeared frequently—in many forms, and in all kinds of circumstances. One of the places he was most likely to appear was at a card game. "The Devil is in the 45s," was how one woman expressed it. And, of all his disguises, perhaps the most common was that of a large black dog.

One night, in the western part of the Island, a group of men were playing cards for chickens and ducks. In the midst of the game, a serious argument developed and it appeared as though a fight were about to break out. At that moment someone noticed a large black dog lying under one of the chairs. As soon as his presence was detected, he jumped up and leaped through the wall without leaving a hole.

One of the peculiarities of human nature is that any taboo becomes, in exact ratio to the strength of the prohibition, a source of fascination and temptation. Thus, an encounter with the Devil became for some a titillating, forbidden fruit, as is seen in a story told me about an incident alleged to have occurred in the Freetown area.

The high July sun beat down mercilessly on the backs of four brothers as they sullenly hoed their way up seemingly endless rows of turnips. They had been at it since early in the morning and their boyish spirits sagged in the midday heat. A fifth brother was not present and the four workers were vexed by his absence. He was an accomplished escape artist when it came to unpleasant tasks around the farm and the four boys sweltered, not just from the heat, but also from anger at his unfair defection.

Late morning they spied him, sauntering up the back lane in their direction. They hoped he might be coming with some cold water and a lunch, and that he would share the work for the rest of the day. Sure enough, he had the food and water, and soon all five of them were sprawled under a tree as only boys escaping work can sprawl. But the prodigal brother had no intention of submitting to the tedium of an afternoon in the turnip patch. His nimble mind went to work. "I dare you," he said, "to hoe those turnips in the name of the Devil."

There was a moment of suspended silence, but soon the boys, happy for any diversion, began to enter into the spirit of the dare. "Let's do it," they cried in youthful defiance, "let's hoe the damned turnips in the name of old Nick." They loitered a little longer and then went back to work, temporarily rejuvenated by the thrill of their own audacity, while the scheming brother sat laughing in the grass. But the good humour ended abruptly. "I can't see," exclaimed one brother. "Neither can I," whimpered another, then another, and another. The four sacrilegious little turnip hoers had all gone blind, and it was a terrified and deeply repentant fifth brother who led them home to Ma. The horse was hastily hitched and the boys taken off to the priest in Summerfield. After much prayer and a liberal application of holy water they regained their sight. Thoroughly chastened they drove home in silence to face the fury of their outraged mother.

A short distance behind the wagon loped a large black dog which disappeared mysteriously when they turned up the lane.

Moonblindness

It was a night of lunar glory.

The full moon streamed through the young man's window in procession, and once he got up and just stared out the window, amazed and enraptured. There were layers of clouds drifting by, and the light, reflecting and re-reflecting, created great illuminated heavenly chambers which moved off to the east and gradually disappeared into the darkness. There was one in particular, so perfectly radiant and celestial that it seemed more a vision than a mere viewing.

A long dark cloud shaped like a fox nosed underneath and passed by stealthily to some other place. Then a large, heavy clot of blackness moved in. He felt a panic as the moon slid underneath and disappeared entirely. Darkness. The silver landscape gone. But only for a few moments, and in the reappearing a deep joy welled up in him.

When he went outside in the morning the cattle in the field were dazed and groggy. Some of them staggered. They seemed intoxicated. He was alarmed, and when an elderly neighbour came by he asked him to come and have a look. "Nothin' to fret about," the old man assured him, "it's just a case of moonblindness. Sometimes when the moon is full like it was last night it affects the cattle, you know. Puts them under a kind of spell. But don't worry about it, they'll come around soon."

The old man proceeded to recount how, when he was a boy, all the old people believed in the moon: how they'd plant by the moon, cut grain and longers by the moon, even pull yellow weeds by the moon. "Certain times of the moon," he said, "they'd kill a pig. Wrong time and the pork would all shrivel up in the pan, but the right time and it would fry out level." As he spoke he moved his flattened hand across in front of him in a gesture of indisputable confirmation.

Later in the day another man came by—a skeptic. "Moonblindness," he scoffed, "that sounds to me like an old country superstition. They've probably gotten into some ragwort or other bad weed."

It seemed reasonable, but to the young man's surprise, he experienced a kind of resentment, as if he himself had been somehow diminished by the other man's dismissive comments. And though he wasn't sure what to think, something deep inside told him that moonblindness was his preferred explanation.

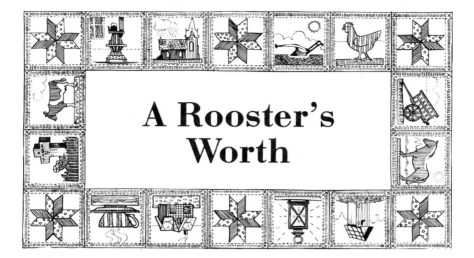

A Rooster's Worth

It was what you would call a barter economy. There wasn't much money in circulation, so instead of buying with cash you traded with goods and services: a few bags of potatoes for a barrel of herring, or a day in the woods for a day at the threshing. You might do business for an entire year at the local store and never so much as catch sight of a dollar bill. You just traded what you had for what you needed, and at the end of the year the merchant would tally up and you would settle up.

In that largely self-sufficient subsistence society, the "boughten" goods required were few. Sugar, salt, molasses, tea, a bit of ginger, or a pair of boots were some of the commodities you couldn't produce on the farm. If you had money you might pay for them, but often you bartered. You could barter with butter, or, in late summer, you might barter with blueberries. Eggs, a goose, a quilt or mat, socks or mitts, a bag of carrots, or a heifer on the hoof—these were just some of the articles of trade in that exchange system. On January 3, 1910, Andrew MacLeod from Irishtown left this account in his diary: "Killed 12 chickens in forenoon, went to Malpeque in afternoon, took 12 chickens, one tub of butter and one ox hide." In return MacLeod received "one box of raisins, one pair of rubbers, socks for Heath [his son], and 30 pounds of sugar." He seemed satisfied with the trade.

Trading goods at the local store was the most common type of barter, but the practice was more widespread than that. I read of one man who paid his bill at the blacksmith with forty-four pounds of fox meat and the use of a pasture the following summer. In that same ledger there was an entry indicating that one customer settled up with a "molasses puncheon" and a "junk of pig." I know of another man who, in the heyday of the Island fox industry, walked into one of the early car dealerships in Summerside with some pelts on his back and traded them on the spot for a new automobile. Many country women exchanged the winter's production of hooked mats to the itinerant "matman" for a "square" of linoleum. I recall as well the story of a man from the Alberton area—I think his name was Foley—who was out of cash and needing gas for his old car. Nothing daunted, he went out to the barnyard, grabbed a rooster, and drove to the gas station. When he was asked by the man at the pump how much he wanted, he is alleged to have pulled the bird out from behind the seat and said, "I'd like a rooster's worth."

The doctor and the minister, whether they liked it or not, were often paid with produce of one kind or another. The yard of one doctor in Crapaud was always strewn with piles of hardwood. He would deliver a baby, and the father would deliver a load of wood. Doctor Preston MacIntyre from Montague confirmed this in conversation. "People sometimes paid me with produce," he explained, "apples and things like that, chickens, turnips, and wood, oh yeah, yeah, and even moonshine sometimes." On occasion the doctor didn't even get that much. Doctor Roddie MacDonald from St. Peter's, who had a very long practice, was asked one day if he was ever paid for delivering a certain baby. "Hhrumph," he retorted, "I still haven't gotten paid for the grandfather."

Another unusual form of barter was the naming of a child after the physician. One old-time doctor said he always hated it when he heard that a boy child was being christened with his name. In his experience that meant he probably wouldn't receive his fee.

There was one kind of barter in this province which was our own version of the black market. I am referring to the illegal but very common practice of trading your vote for a bottle of rum, or, for non-imbibers, a crisp new five-dollar bill. In a close election, the law of supply and demand would inflate the value of your franchise and I heard of one shrewd woman who demanded for her vote a new kitchen chrome set and a case of Carnation milk. I don't know whether she got them, but I doubt she settled for five dollars.

Of all the items traded, eggs were easily the most common commodity. In many homes all the purchased groceries for the family were provided in this manner, and there were many youngsters from farm families who were put through college with the egg money. Also, when there was no cash in your purse or pocket, eggs became the currency of last resort. A woman from the Stanley Bridge area had nothing whatever for her young daughter's birthday. She solved the problem by giving the girl a dozen eggs to take for trade to the local store. The girl, recalling the incident, said she had no idea of the value of the eggs, but picked out candy from behind the glass until the shopkeeper informed her that all her money—or eggs—were spent.

Another incident from the Woodstock area involved a group of five boys who decided one afternoon they would buy a fig of twist tobacco between them. A fig cost five cents and each agreed he would bring one cent to school the next day. In the morning four of the boys arrived with the money, but one hadn't been able to get a penny so he came with an egg. In remembering the episode he said that the old lady who ran the store took the egg outside and sighted it against the sun to be sure it was fresh. It was, and the boys got the twist—but soon wished they hadn't. They became deathly sick and at least one of them never chewed again in his life.

I think the best egg story I ever heard was about the woman who wanted to go to a dance, but had no money for the small admission charge. The merchant in that area would take goods in barter but, apparently, if he did not have the items requested he would give you the cash. The woman, determined to get out for a night of jigs and reels, hatched a scheme. She had heard just the day before that the storekeeper was out of sleigh bolts, so she sent her son to the store with a tray of eggs and advised him sternly that, under no circumstances, was he to settle for anything except some bolts. She then set about ironing her best dress for the anticipated recreation. What she didn't realize was that an order of sleigh bolts had come in on the morning train.

To her great dismay, her son arrived home with a bag of bolts. As he ran into the house he laughingly cried out, "Sorry, Mom, no dancin' tonight."

Count 'em, Belle

Doctor Preston MacIntyre from Montague once told me that he had personally delivered all seventeen children in one family. "Yes," he quipped, with a bit of a grin, "and some of them were better than twelve pounds!" He estimated that during his career he had delivered approximately 5,500 babies.

It was an era of large households. A family with four or five children was considered small. If there were only two or three, everyone wondered why, and the priest might make it his business to find out. More common were families of eight or ten, or even fourteen or sixteen. One woman I heard about had twenty-three, and I suspect a bit of checking might reveal that she doesn't hold the record. A man from Clinton recalled a family of fourteen children. The father once told him that he wouldn't take a million dollars for any one of them, but that he wouldn't give two cents for another.

In a family that large it could be difficult just to keep track of everyone. A woman from St. Peter's Island used to dress up her large brood and take them to church in the wagon across the sand flats to Nine Mile Creek. When she would be gathering them up after the service, the minister would say, "Count 'em, Belle! Count 'em! See if you've got 'em all."

I sometimes try to imagine the scene at mealtimes in those homes where there would be a dozen or more crowded around the large wooden kitchen table. Sadie Roberts, who had ten brothers

45

and one sister, described the scene at breakfast. "I set the table first, fourteen places. One small plate and one large plate. And then I would go around and give out the oatmeal for fourteen people." Another individual from an especially large family remembered with some irritation all the times he had to wait for "the second round," and a woman told me recently that, in her uncle's house, the boys ate first.

Sleeping arrangements were also complex. There would often be three or four in one bed, which lent a whole new meaning to the word bedlam. One man who survived this experience recalled that in the bed he shared, "There would be some sleepin' with their heads at one end and some at the other," and that the surest way to get trouble started was to "stick your feet in the other fella's face." When that happened, he said, "the war would be on."

Eldest daughters in these large families were frequently called upon to assume a heavy weight of responsibility. Some of them would be making meals, baking bread, and caring for infants while other girls their age were still playing with dolls or skipping rope in the yard. One woman, the oldest of fourteen, said, "It seemed every time I sat down I had a child on my knee." She claimed she was glad to do it for her beleaguered mother but admitted that sometimes it made her sad. She remembered one occasion when she was sitting in the window, feeding a baby, and watching other children coasting on a nearby hill. "Even to this day," she said, "when I think of that I still get this lonesome feeling."

Many hands made light work, but it was also true that many mouths to feed, many diapers to change, many lessons to supervise, many cuts and scrapes to tend, and many tears to dry made for much work—especially for the mothers. One woman, mother of fourteen, said the day her youngest started school was the first day she heard the clock tick.

The Great Taboo

For Roman Catholics, the ideal was to be celibate, like Jesus, the Apostle Paul, or perhaps like the priest, or the sisters at the convent. If that wasn't possible, the next best thing was to have a celibate mind, which meant you didn't think or talk about sex. Protestant teaching was formally somewhat less severe, but that didn't mean you were liable to hear a sermon on the joy of sex or be encouraged to turn to the erotic "Song of Solomon" for your devotional reading. In both camps, human sexual activity tended to be regarded as a necessary evil.

From the earliest days of tribal existence, humans have been attempting to control and domesticate the potentially disruptive power of sexual energy. It was no different on the Island. The strategy here was to render it a largely shameful, unspeakable thing to be pushed out of sight and eliminated from conversation. It was a strategy of suppression, supported by the myth of original sin and the Augustinian/Calvinist conception of life which emphasized a sharp separation between a higher and lower nature. Sex couldn't be denied altogether, but it could be assigned to that carnal lower region, and I sometimes think it ironic that those farming people, whose hands were so often in the earth or the bread dough, were constrained to live so uneasily with the soil and yeast of their own natures.

The consequence of all this was that boys and girls were kept in the dark. They taught you about making bread and making hay, but no one ever said anything about making love. When it came to understanding the mystery of your own emergent sexuality, you were pretty much on your own, and if you got your education "out behind the barn," it was almost certainly from an inexperienced or uncaring tutor. As a child you learned very early to guard carefully your most private thoughts and feelings, and never let anything show that would invite the scourge of barbed-wire tongues.

A friend, now in her sixties, told me only recently about a painful episode from her girlhood. She smiles about it now, but it was evident in her telling that it was a difficult memory. When she was seventeen she was kissed by a boy at her home. "He put his lips on my mouth" was, I believe, the way she described it. It was just a kiss, and scarcely that, but it created in her a deep ensuing fear: the fear that she might have become pregnant. She also confided that the incident was the cause of a prolonged depression, and a factor in her subsequent decision to enter a convent where she remained for three years. "It made me hate my own body," was her sad recollection.

An unlikely story? Not at all. Like many others at that time, she had been told absolutely nothing about sex. Words like menstruation, intercourse, and, God forbid, masturbation were completely off-limits. Come to think of it, I was probably in my teens before I realized that there were actual names for genitalia, other than those employed in schoolyard talk. There was such a taboo surrounding the entire subject that it was not uncommon for a woman, or a man, or both, to climb apprehensively into bed on their wedding night without ever having had a conversation with anyone about sexual behaviour or human reproduction. "Sex was a forbidden subject," recalled another woman. "I came from a family of six older brothers and lived on a farm, but it simply was not talked about. I remember when I first saw the word 'sex' in a book, even that was embarrassing."

The fact that "it" could scarcely be talked about was, in itself, a message. Though little was said, what was communicated in the hushing up was that sex was something shameful. A woman who grew up in the 1930s said, "All children received the message from parents, community, and church that anything related to sex was sinful, bad, and dirty. Even to see a pregnant woman was something to be embarrassed about."

When I was living in Murray Harbour I was acquainted with an elderly man who had a unique way of responding to the question, "How are you today?" When he met someone at the store or in the foyer of the church and they asked him how he was, he would respond, "Pretty straight." It was, as I now see it, a perfect description of the society of his experience: a hard-working, hand-to-mouth society where there was little margin for error and, consequently, a suspicion of spontaneity or frivolity of any kind. You could see it in the austere line of their architecture, in the geometry of their quilt and mat patterns, in the fence lines that divided their fields, and in the people themselves. Everything was "pretty straight," and anything that wasn't was pretty well kept out of sight.

But pregnancy was a problem, being an indisputable visual attestation to the fact that sexual activity had occurred. The obvious solution was to keep pregnant women out of sight, and that's just what happened. A woman who was "that way" or "expecting" would sometimes curtail or even discontinue altogether her appearances in public. Even within the home, attempts would be made to disguise the pregnancy from the children for as long as possible. A married teacher who became pregnant was asked to resign immediately, before she began to show. One woman said that when she was a teenager her mother, to her surprise, appeared downstairs one day with a new baby. Though living under the same roof, she didn't know until the day of the birth that her mother was expecting. And, when an unmarried girl became pregnant, it was calamitous. It meant banishment. If she were not confined to an upstairs bedroom she would almost certainly be sent upstairs when company arrived. Often she was sent right out of the province, sometimes never to return.

An Acadian woman from Egmont Bay was reflecting on the customs and rituals surrounding marriage in her younger years. "When the bride and groom were finally united in holy matrimony, it was," she recalled, "a sin to kiss. It was not allowed under any circumstances on the altar." Although she didn't realize it, she was describing the sex education of her day. There wasn't much information dispensed, but what was communicated was a powerful message which connected guilt and depravity with human sexuality. One eighty-five-year-old woman from Georgetown expressed this with charming alacrity. "Oh blessed angels!" she exclaimed, "that wasn't heard of. You didn't hear about those things.... Holy Mother, no, they wouldn't even talk about that!"

A very great modesty was an understandable by-product of that sexually uncomfortable society. I know, for example, that in some communities there was a definite decorum required in hanging out the wash. Women's bloomers, the old square type, were folded over a couple of times on the line so they would look like a dish towel. You didn't have to be quite so careful with the men's undergarments. It was, I suppose, a kind of wash-day declaration of the double standard. Although long johns didn't have to be disguised as a pillow slip or a table cloth, it was considered risqué to hang them out without first buttoning the flap at the back. I suspect, moreover, that some women did a quick check through the window from time to time. You couldn't be too careful. On a windy day there was always the danger the flap would blow open.

The Mixed Marriage

I t usually went something like this: boy met girl, boy courted girl, boy and girl fell in love, and then they got married. Now we all know it's seldom that simple, and on Prince Edward Island if the boy was a Roman Catholic, and the girl a Protestant—or the other way around—it most certainly was not that simple. It could be sour enough if one was a Baptist and the other a Presbyterian or Methodist, but if one was a Protestant and the other a Roman Catholic, it was almost impossible. It was a tragedy, that's what it was.

Because of the prevailing attitudes, families—even communities—could be torn apart by a single matrimonial mishap. The young man and woman might fall in love, but they soon discovered they had fallen into a whole lot more than that. Many parents lived in dread of a mixed courtship all the time their children were growing up, and, if they got word that a son or daughter was keeping company with one of "the wrong kind," they moved in pretty fast to prevent the disaster of a mixed marriage.

But they weren't always successful. The mating instinct often proved greater and more patient than the power of prohibition and bigotry. One widowed woman had a daughter in her twenties who fell in love with a Roman Catholic man. They wanted to marry but the old matriarch would have none of it. "No, no," she protested, "definitely not! Not over my dead body!" Over the next twenty-five years the couple met secretly. When the old woman finally died, her daughter's ineligible suitor was a pallbearer at her funeral. Then he married her daughter.

One Island boy went out west to work and never returned. He never even wrote, just disappeared. Months later the worried father travelled across the country to locate his lost son, and found him. The boy had married a Roman Catholic girl and was afraid to go home or to write with such devastating news.

A Roman Catholic woman recalled that whenever she brought a boy home, her mother would ask him nonchalantly if his mother belonged to the C.W.L. (Catholic Women's League). Another, also a Roman Catholic, said that she grew up right next to a Protestant community and that, as a teenager, she was solemnly advised by her parents, "not even to look in that direction."

There was a small glossary of words and phrases which grew up around this subject of "the mixed marriage." One Protestant girl told me she was talking to her grandfather about her boyfriend and happened to mention his name. "Oh," he retorted, "he's *one of those*, is he? Why can't you find *one of your own kind?*" The word "turned" was also common. A man had this to say about changing religions because of marriage: "It was shameful, really, like changin' the colour of your skin, or your sex, or something. I guess you could never be trusted if you turned." But the one I like best is from a fellow who said, "As far as the Catholics were concerned, if you were a Protestant you were going to hell, and I'm half-Protestant, so I know." Where else, I wonder, would a person think to describe himself as "half-Protestant." But it's entirely logical. On the Island, religion was in your genes, and a mixed marriage produced a spiritual hybrid: half-Protestant, half-Roman Catholic.

Growing up in today's more benign religious environment, a kind of ecumenical potpourri of tolerance and easy-going acceptance, many young people can scarcely imagine the intensity of the old sectarian feelings in that pre-Vatican II society. It produced a great amount of suspicion and ill will, and many casualties. It was difficult to rise above it, for tolerance in that climate was almost certain to be interpreted as a sign of doctrinal deviance or family betrayal.

There was one woman from down east who managed to cut through all that. She had a boyfriend of "the wrong kind," so didn't marry him, just lived common law for years and years. One day the priest came by and suggested she do the right thing and get married. "Dear God, Father!" she responded in mock astonishment, "you're not suggesting I marry him. He's Protestant, you know."

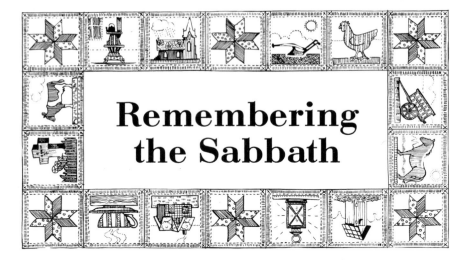

Remembering the Sabbath

Remember the Sabbath Day to keep it Holy! These words once resonated with great authority in this province. The appropriate observation of Sunday, known to many as the Christian Sabbath, was a matter of compelling importance, a sign and test of true piety.

In speaking to old people, I have discovered that there are two Sabbaths in their memory: the negative Sabbath, and the positive Sabbath. The one was a day of strict prohibition; the other, a day of blessing. The grim keepers of the negative Sabbath were those who supposed that strict Sunday decorum was necessary to stay on the good side of a scolding and somewhat dyspeptic deity. It was His day, and He wanted it all to Himself. In one community there were several children from one family who turned out rather poorly, bringing sorrow and disgrace to their parents. In attempting to understand this sad state of affairs, there were those who came to the remarkable conclusion that it must have had something to do with the neglect of proper Sabbath observation in their home.

The keepers of the positive Sabbath had a different, sunnier view. For them, the day of rest was a precious thing, a gift out of the goodness of God's kindly nature. You get a sense of this in the old saying, "Come day, go day, God send Sunday." In a world of unremitting labour, the Sabbath was for them an oasis of rest, a time for the healing of weary and workworn bodies, and the mending of the spirit. It was a day, not of recreation, but of re-creation.

Both groups were extremely vigilant about keeping the Sabbath: the first because they feared the consequences of displeasing God or of scandalizing their neighbours, the second because they understood how easily human compulsion and greed could ruin a good thing. And so there had to be rules. Very strict rules.

Those unfamiliar with this earlier era might suppose that keeping the Sabbath was quite a simple thing. That was far from the case. There was an elaborate code of laws and loopholes—a kind of unwritten Protestant Talmud—to cover every imaginable circumstance. It was permitted, for example, to pick berries off the plant and eat them out of your hand, but you couldn't put them in a dish or dipper. That was work. And when the Sunday dinner was finished it was permissible to wash the fine china, but not the everyday dishes. That, apparently, was also work. And as you stood around after church and chatted with your neighbours, you might talk about crops or livestock, but you didn't talk prices.

The same fine-tuning of the Sabbath law was apparent in the handling of a situation in one home where, on Sunday afternoon, it was discovered that no one had remembered to cut any kindling. What would they do? They could not split wood on the holy day, but if no wood were split, how was supper to be prepared for the guests? Out of this high drama a creative solution emerged. After much soul-searching, the father whispered to one of the boys, "Son, go out and break up a bit of wood with the back of the axe."

But how were children to understand all that? For them, the concept of Sabbath must have been bewildering. My wife's grandmother recalled walking across a winter field with her father on a Sunday afternoon. When she came to a little patch of ice, she ran and slid across it. Her father, not an unkind man, soon put a stop to it. "Tut, tut, child," he said in gentle reprimand, "not on the Sabbath, not on the Sabbath."

The theological implications of the episode are weighty. God must have seemed a very great crank to have been upset by that short slide between frozen furrows. Relationship with such an irritable Being, however holy His nature, would never be easy, a fact borne out in the lives of many of my Presbyterian friends and acquaintances. It occurs to me, however, that in many instances God really didn't have much to do with it. In that society of watchful, curious neighbours, there was always more to consider than the pleasure or opprobrium of the Almighty. One woman who would never put out a wash on Sunday would sometimes sneak a tablecloth or dish towel over a rose-bush behind the porch. When it was pointed out to her that God could see it there as easily as on the line, she replied with perfect candour, "It's not God I'm worried about, but the neighbours!"

Makes you wonder, doesn't it? Perhaps it wasn't God who was so cranky in the first place.

Big Feelin'

There was a tyranny which operated in that outwardly mild, populist society which existed on Prince Edward Island before "the break"; a kind of communal bullying which kept you in your place. It was, if you will, the tyranny of egalitarianism.

There was comfort in knowing that all your neighbours were in pretty much the same situation as you were. You might not have much yourself, but at least you knew that others had the same. It seemed fair, and made it easier to accept privation and limitation. The shadow side of this was that it produced a powerful disincentive to exceptionality of any kind. If you showed any serious inclination to rise above your station or do things differently, you were liable to feel the cold hand of community disapproval pulling you back down to where you belonged. And, if you persisted in your presumption, there would be many just waiting to see you crash so they could celebrate your fall.

You can sense something of this in the comments of a sixty-seven-year-old retired farmer from Kings County who said he "never much liked people who were overbearing or conceited. Most people," he continued, "didn't want much to do with those who were really big on themselves. If you wanted to be liked and accepted you were kind of decent to everyone else, like everyone else was to you." The part about being decent to others seems harmless enough, but I'm a little suspicious about the reference to those who were "big on themselves." Self-effacement, whether sincere or not, was an acceptable, even desirable character trait; but you had to be careful about self-confidence. The surest way to estrange yourself from the community, apart from committing some unspeakable crime, was to be "big on yourself."

If you were too ambitious, too clever, too outspoken, too pushy, or too well-off, you were in trouble. Fitting in was the important thing, and being "too this" or "too that" made you stand out, arousing the suspicion that you thought yourself better than your peers. People were really touchy about that. As one man put it, "Even if you were doing well you were supposed to act as though you were livin' from one barrel of fish to the next."

The person in political life had to be especially aware of this levelling instinct in his fellow Islanders. It is common knowledge in Prince Edward Island that a politician who flies too high will soon have his wings clipped. I recall one very successful veteran politician advising a group of younger colleagues in caucus that they shouldn't give anyone reason to believe they had changed in any way just because they had been elected. "They'll soon bring you down to earth," he reminded them gravely.

In this province we often seem more comfortable with failure than success. We know how to handle it better. We have the skills. Success, on the other hand, is awkward, abnormal, disturbing. It can damn a person, especially if the individual has the bad sense to reveal in any way that he is aware of his success. It leaves you open to that most devastating of all criticisms, that you have become "big feelin'."

I know one student from a rural district who confessed that he was worried about being educated, and getting a university degree. He just knew in his bones that it would create a problem back home, and possibly alienate him from his own family. "Islanders are a jealous breed," he observed, "and one of your own would be the first to tear you down." Such attitudes, of course, had a solid theological underpinning. God was routinely depicted as being tremendously insecure, an avenging spirit who regarded any sign of self-assertion or "big-feelin'" as a threat to his precarious majesty. Insecure worshippers of such a deity were able to feel absolutely virtuous about their own jealousy and judgementalism. Keeping others in their place was, it seemed, merely an imitation of the divine nature.

Being too sure about anything could also leave you open to the charge of being "big feelin'." It's one of the reasons the entire

Courtesy Jane Brammer

province acquired the reputation of being so "laid back," and why
many of the old-timers were so understated and indirect. They knew
how easily they could give offence by giving advice.

I recall the time I was helping my father-in-law, Ralph Roberts,
build a small barn. We were working on the roof when we noticed
the old farmer from across the field standing in the barnyard watching the proceedings with apparent interest. After a bit, Ralph, who
obviously understood the hidden dynamic of the moment, climbed
down the ladder and went over to talk to his neighbour. After ex-
changing some small talk about how quickly the structure was going
up and how useful it would be, the topic of the roof was gently ne-
gotiated into the conversation. The old man, who had built a barn or
two in his life, made some general comments about how a roofline
which was perfectly plumb would appear otherwise from the road,
and hinted it might be a good idea to make allowance for that in the
construction. There were a few more pleasantries, and then he am-
bled on home. When Ralph returned to the roof, I asked him what
was going on. "Lem had some advice for us," he reported, "but I
practically had to coax it out of him."

I have a friend, a product of that rural regime, whose speech is
so modified by qualification and reservation that he always seems to
be defending himself against some internalized adversary who

might jump on his statements at any moment and accuse him of being too opinionated or too sure of himself. He is articulate and witty, but much of the time seems incapable of saying anything precisely. You would gather from his talk that he is never quite sure what he thinks, what he wants, or where he is going. The words "possibly," "maybe," "perhaps," and "suppose" are never far from his tongue, and when he says "probably," you know he is in an especially assertive mood. There are times when he strings a number of these qualifiers together in a dazzling display of tentativeness. This man loves a drink, but driving in the car with him one day I heard him say, "Do you suppose maybe it might be a good idea to stop and get a little beer? What do you think?"

I think perhaps he wanted some beer.

Happy as a Clam

I sn't it strange how certain things people say will stick with you, like an arrow lodged in the mind. It was years ago and I was visiting with Silas and Bertha MacKay at their home in Beach Point. It was probably over one of Bertha's incomparable roast beef dinners that Silas was talking about a boat someone had made. "She was well put together," he said, "as tight as a cup." I had never heard that saying before, but it seemed to me a stroke of brilliance. Who could ever forget such an apt turn of phrase: "as tight as a cup." It was perfect; immortal. An arrow had landed.

Silas was a man who would surprise you with his comparisons. He probably had never heard of a simile, but he used them all the time; which, to my way of thinking, is a lot further ahead than knowing what they are but not being able to use them. I confess, for example, that if I were attempting to describe something extra heavy I'd be liable to say, "heavy as a rock." On a bad day, I might even say, "heavy as lead," and be ashamed afterwards. But Silas could always do better than that. I remember once he was describing something he had carried. It was, he said, "as heavy as a man and a boy."

I call to mind another time he was telling me how one person had rudely interrupted another in conversation. "He cut him off like a carrot," was the way he put it. I mean, you could learn to talk from a man like that. I don't know if Silas coined any of these himself. Probably not. More likely they were passed down to him from the old people: verbal heirlooms, to be used, and then passed on to the next generation like a fancy vase or a fine tool.

Folk language was full of these apt comparisons. Some of them were ordinary, but the ones which survived the winnowing process of repeated usage were the work of genius, requiring often a real leap of imagination. Consider, for example, the saying, "as busy as a fart in a mitt." I confess I can scarcely imagine anyone clever enough to have thought that up. Perhaps it was an accident. But there were many others: "as bold as a pet pig," "as wide as a fishcake," "as old as the fog," "all dressed up like a spare bedroom," "flatter than piss on a plate," "as clumsy as a bag of hammers," "as mean as the white end of goose shit," and, "as happy as a clam."

This last one intrigues me. I really have no idea why anyone would think to say, "as happy as a clam." The attempt to understand it is futile, like trying to explain a joke. But I know in my heart it is perfect. In other words, it's "as right as rain."

In this present age of surface descriptions and literal, one-dimensional conversation, these sayings, and hundreds of others like them, are reminders of the evocative oral commerce of that disappeared folk culture. They recall a time when metaphor was the key to wisdom, and imagination more important than mere information. And anyone who can't see that is "as stupid as pissin' the bed awake."

The Party Line

I sometimes find it difficult to believe that we have all submitted, voluntarily, to that very great invasion of our privacy and peace which is the telephone, the most rude and intrusive of all human inventions. I suppose it speaks profoundly of our desire to be in touch with one another, and of our need for relationship, but I am still surprised by our obeisance to this noisy little package of technology. Some people have one in every room, and one they can take with them to the yard or in the car, as though the telephone was the very life-source itself.

I recall with even greater amazement that in the early days of the telephone there might be twenty or thirty, or even forty or fifty families on a single party line. The ringing was constant.

Ring! Ring! Ring!

"Margaret, was that our ring?"

"No, that was Will's ring, two long and one short."

"Are you sure?"

"Yes, I'm positive. But if it was ours they will try again."

Ring! Ring! Ring!

And so it went, an unremitting jangle of ringing-in, ringing-out, and ringing-over. The isolation of rural life was overcome but, alas! the serenity of the countryside was forever shattered.

For the eavesdropper and the gossipmonger, whose numbers were not small, the telephone was a gift from heaven. It delivered right into the privacy of your home that most precious and delectable of all rural commodities—the news of the neighbours.

Ahh! the party line. What an institution! A source of information, but also of recreation and vexation. The recreation for many was the common practice of "listening-in." The vexation was hearing all those clicks on the line, each of which announced the presence of yet another auditor to your conversation.

I suppose everyone gave in to the temptation now and then, but there were others who gave in to the temptation every time the phone rang. They were the heavy-duty eavesdroppers and whenever you talked on the phone, day or night, you could be sure that they were there, silent partners on every call. You might hear their clock ticking, or their dog bark, and in time you learned to identify them by their breathing. You knew they were on the line, but you couldn't get them off. You might even resort to calling them by name in an attempt to shame them into hanging up.

"Good afternoon, Ida. I know you're there. Now would you please go get supper for Fred."

But it usually didn't work. They would not so easily be denied their pleasure. There was a family up west where listening-in was a common pastime; so common, indeed, that the woman of the house made a tiny, finely embroidered cushion which fit perfectly into the stationary, trumpet-shaped mouthpiece. It effectively muted any tell-tale noises from her household, which meant she could relax and put up her feet while eavesdropping.

These news-gatherers regarded every ring as their ring, and I was told of one woman who would lie down on the kitchen lounge every night after supper and spend the evening just waiting for the calls. Apparently she once told a friend that if there was anything personal she would hang up immediately.

Now why do I find that so difficult to believe?

Leapo

There are few of the old, steep-pitched, one-room school-houses still standing around the countryside. Most have been hauled away, torn down, or renovated beyond recognition, though some remain, solitary and dilapidated, like aged veterans from some great war. There is one on the highway between Rose Valley and Kinkora which always seems to me an especially forlorn sight, perhaps because it still retains its old faded sign above the door: SHAMROCK AND THISTLE. It speaks of desertion, as though one day everyone just walked out and never returned.

I never pass that little building without recalling schoolyard scenes of years ago. In my ear of recollection I hear sing-song voices drifting across the decades, the voices of children playing games at noontime. And it is my own voice I hear, and my own name being shouted. How quickly we would eat our simple noon lunch—the bread, the round cookie, and the small bottle of milk with waxed paper under the cover—so we could rush out into the schoolyard and disappear into the wondrous fourth dimension of childhood play. Soon we would be lost in the games, like creatures in a dream, until the obscene bell would call us back: back into the school, back into our seats, back, alas, into time.

I don't know where all those games came from, or who taught us, but as I think back, it occurs to me that many of them had wonderfully musical names. There was "King King Come Along," "Bull Bull Break the Ring," "Red Rover Red Rover," "Thorny Thorny Weather, Catch a Feather," and, for rainy days, "Billy Billy Button,

Courtesy Harold MacLeod

Who's Got the Button." But of all the games we played in the schoolyard, there is one which stands out in memory more clearly than the rest. At our school in Greenmount we called it "leapo," while in other, more prosaic communities, it was known simply as "leap."

How I loved that game! The entire school would divide into two teams which would take their places, one on either side of the schoolhouse. Someone would begin the game by throwing a sponge rubber ball over the schoolhouse while crying out, "Leapo!" If the ball didn't make it over the peak he would immediately cry out, "Oh no!" and try again. In my mind those two—"Leapo! Oh no!"—still run together like a chant.

When the toss was successful, the children on the receiving side would attempt to catch the ball before it hit the ground. The boy or girl who made the catch would then run around the building and throw the ball at the frantically fleeing opponents. The high drama, of course, was the uncertainty of whether your adversary would suddenly burst on the scene from the left or from the right, and those few seconds of waiting were charged with an almost unbearable tension. You could play it safe and stay in the middle, or you could gamble and move to one side. If you guessed right you were certain of escape, but if you guessed wrong you were a sitting duck. If you were struck or "plugged" by the thrown ball, you suffered the disgrace of having to join the other team.

It might seem rather primitive, yet it contained all the elements of action, suspense, and simulated danger which are present in most good games. Even as I write, I am once again that earnest, scab-kneed little boy, eyes fixed intently on the peak of the roof, all poised and waiting for the summoning cry: "Leee-po!"

Waste Not, Want Not

S ome people called it "being careful," and when I talk to older
Islanders it soon becomes apparent that one of the pre-emi-
nent virtues of their lives was the virtue of frugality. In that era
of scarcity, when the gross annual income from some farms was less
than five hundred dollars—and fishing brought even less—you had
to hold on tightly to every cent.

Frugality was like a religion, inasmuch as it was for many the
central guiding principle of their lives. It might not save your soul,
but it inspired you to save everything else. A "saving person" was
vigilant and abstemious, always on guard against the demon of extravagance and the ruin it could bring; or, as one elderly woman told
me, "Father made me see that you can't give way to extravagance. No
you just can't give way to it."

"Wilful waste makes woeful want," was a principle of life rank-
ing right up there with the golden rule, and indebtedness a condition
more to be feared than a state of mortal sin. "Don't buy anything on
Monday or you will be spending all week," was a revered proverb in
that kingdom of carefulness, as was the shorter, though no less omi-
nous, "Waste not, want not." These were more than tidy little apho-
risms. They were maxims by which men and women regulated their
entire existence. Making, making over, and making do was how they
lived.

68

As in any religion there were fanatics—a kind of lunatic fringe where the virtue of "being careful" crossed over the line into being "mean," or "tight." Some people were so much in the grip of this compulsion that it really hurt them to throw anything away or to spend a dollar. One man told me about a farmer in his community who would literally turn his back when he was paying someone for a day's work. He figured the man found it too disturbing to witness the money changing hands. Another man always had his wife pay the help.

These people were close to the line, but there were others who went over—way over. A man in the Summerside area was reputed to be extremely close with his pennies. When he eventually married, after doubtless considering carefully the cost benefits of the arrangement, he decided to go to Halifax on the train for a honeymoon of sorts. But to save money he chose not to take his bride. When questioned about this unusual decision, he hastened to explain that she had already been there once. But the man who outdid all others, a true pillar-saint in the pantheon of frugality, was an old man from Charlottetown. It is alleged that in the evening he would sit with his trousers pulled down round his knees to save the wear and tear on the seat of his pants. It's hard to beat that.

It might seem to most of us a rather joyless creed, this religion of thrift, with its austere doctrines of fiscal restraint and compulsive retentiveness. But that wasn't necessarily so. My brother-in-law, Rod Nicholson, told me the story of a man who, through careful management and the avoidance of extravagance, had accumulated by the end of his life a tidy sum of money. An acquaintance, feeling sorry for the old man, suggested it might be time for him to "get some good" out of his savings, and reminded him that he would have to leave it to someone who might squander it. But the old man's faith was not easily shaken. "You're probably right," he responded, "but I just hope they get as much pleasure out of spendin' it as I did out of savin' it."

For many Islanders "them times" were hard times, and in some homes there might be months on end when there was not so much as a penny on the premises. Few starved, but many scrimped, and there were occasions when the sight of a five-dollar bill was enough to elevate the pulse and dilate the pupils. Luxuries or treats were few, and I recall the time I received an entire package of gum from an obviously affluent visitor. I went out to the woods behind our house where I turned it over and over in my hands, astounded at my good fortune.

It is amusing to hear Islanders of an earlier generation telling their children or grandchildren how hard they had it as children, especially when the recounting is flavoured with good-humoured exaggeration. One man said when he was a boy his family was so poor that he and his siblings would draw laces on their bare feet and pretend they had shoes. Another man, tongue in cheek, said his mother used to send him to school with pictures of food in his lunch can. But the one I like best is from a woman who claimed her family was so deprived that she and her sisters would put on their hats and sit in the window watching people travelling by on the road, all the while pretending they were soon going somewhere.

Easily the most famous anecdote of this genre is the "chicken and point" story which I have heard time and time again from many parts of the province. I believe it is derived from an old Irish joke about poor families in Ireland who ate nothing year round except herring and potatoes. When they had no herring they supplemented their meagre diet by imagining that they did. On Prince Edward Island, the "chicken and point" adaptation of the story goes something like this: "When we were young we had a fine meal every Sunday. My mother would put a picture of a chicken above the table and every time we'd take a bite of potatoes we'd point at that picture. That was what we called chicken dinner."

But in most rural homes it was money, not chickens, that was the truly scare commodity. "There was never any money," recalled one man. "For all the work you did you never got paid. There was no money to be paid. Everyone worked and was glad to work, but there was no such thing as money. I didn't know what it was to have money and I didn't know what it was to be hungry."

His comments remind me of the story of the two fishermen from the Miminegash area who were returning to harbour after a most unsuccessful day on the water. One of the men began to lament about the poor catch and low prices. "Jesus, Mary, and Joseph," he grumbled, "we've been at this all spring and scarcely a cent to show for it."

"Oh, don't be complainin'," chided the other man, "just be thankful we've got the work."

It is little wonder many older Islanders shake their heads in disbelief at some of the changes which have occurred in our economy. They have experienced work without money, but are genuinely perplexed and offended by the concept of money without work. The present practice of idle adults receiving a cheque in the mail every two weeks or idle children receiving a regular allowance from their parents seems strange, even outrageous, to those who grew up in that largely cashless culture.

For some older Island women the poverty of their childhood is recalled in the memory of flour bag garments. Because of the scarcity of the times, recycling was a way of life. Nothing was ever wasted and there were girls who spent many of their younger years in a shapeless flour bag dress over shapeless flour bag bloomers. A woman from Mount Stewart said she had a neighbour who used to make underwear out of flour bags for her daughter and that people would say, "There goes Mrs. Smith, Darlene, and Robin Hood on their way to church." She also recalled that when Darlene bent over you could see "98 lbs. net wt." written on her backside. Another woman said that when she was a girl her sisters made her a flour bag slip which she took with her when she went to the States to work. "I never did get the 'Robin Hood' completely out of it," she recalled, "but it wore forever." She also confided, "Whenever I thought I was getting too big for my britches I would put on that slip and come down a peg or two."

In all of this I am still unable to decide whether people "them times" were actually poorer than we are now. Money was scarce, but it was not then, as it has become, the calculus of all human endeavour. An unmailed letter might sit on the shelf for a week for want of a two-cent stamp; a woman might head to town on the train with four dollars to do the Christmas shopping; or a child might save all winter to get enough money for ice cream and a ride on the horse-driven swing at the annual summer "tea-party." But were those people poor?

Most of us would call it poverty, but many of the older people have a somewhat different interpretation. They confess readily to the lack of currency, but hasten to add that it didn't necessarily make them feel poor. One person put it like this: "I guess we were poor, but we didn't know it." They also point out that because most of their neighbours were in similar circumstances, there wasn't the same opportunity for invidious comparison which, in our society, can promote a sense of deprivation even in the homes of the affluent.

So we should save our pity. It just isn't appropriate. Scarcity was no more a threat to their happiness than abundance is to ours.

Soil
Sacrament

I n that down-to-earth world of small trodden farms and deep-furrowed perseverance there was an affair with the land—an intimacy and a consummation. Every field was named and known, and like a priest pressing his prayerbeads the kneeling farmer passed the soil through his fingers in an act of consecration and blessing. His life's labour was a participation in the miracle of regeneration, and the contours of his land became, over time, the very contours of faith. The farmer had his way with the land, but it was no less true that, inexorably, the land had its way with the farmer. In the end, the rhythm of ploughing, harrowing, scuffling, and harvesting his fields became a melody and narrative inseparable from the storyline of his own life.

The soil entered you through pores and nostrils. Dust in eye corners, earth stains on collars, sweat tracks down strong backs, and soil lines across creased foreheads and around the tops of gray woollen socks were all signs of the deep symbiotic bond between humans and the nurturing earth. Red soil and red blood mingled and merged in a union too elemental for words, but you knew somehow that the clay which was the land and the clay which was yourself—your hands and feet—was the same clay.

One man said his father would announce proudly, "All my fields are in good heart." For the true farmer, the man of the land, this was a source of deep satisfaction, for the good heart of the farmer rested in the good heart of his fields.

I get a sense from some of the old-timers that they were able to discern the very mood of the land. They were sensitive to its look, its feel, even to its smell. As one farmer recalled, "Oh! the smell of the wet earth. I don't suppose I'll ever forget that. The earth had its own peculiar smells at different times. The smell of the earth you got when you were diggin' potatoes was a different smell altogether from the smell of the earth when you were hoeing turnips and there was a special summer smell comin' off the earth. And of course in the spring of the year, when you were harrowing and seeding, there was yet another smell.... Oh yeah! I remember that."

This communion with the soil was celebrated in a practice which was widespread in this province; a practice which might be described as "the Sabbath sacrament of walking the land." Wilfred MacDonald from Brudenell told me about it, as did Lawson Drake from Meadowbank and numerous others. One man surmised that it was related somehow to the example of Jesus who walked through grain fields with his disciples on the Sabbath. Drake called these Sunday walks "planning expeditions." He said that his father would be poking his hands into the ground to see how the seed was germinating or, later in the year, how the potatoes were coming along. He would also be checking the fences, as well as the level of water in the creek.

But there was more to it than that. Those Sunday afternoon walks over the land were also a time of celebration and mystic identification. In Drake's words: "One of my happiest childhood memories was of those Sunday afternoon walks with Father. It was as though, on that day of rest, he had some special communion with the land. I think that there, in those joyous walks, was born in me the conviction...not only that the land is ours, but that we are the land's."

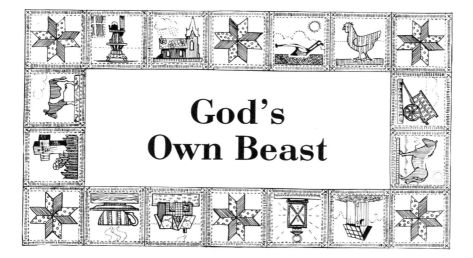

God's
Own Beast

H is name was Jim, aged twenty, and one stormy day in early April, 1950, he plunged and bucked through miles of snow-drifts to deliver my mother to the hospital in Alberton where she gave birth to my sister Barbara. I was along for the trip, hunkered down in some cushioning straw, and have never forgotten that late winter odyssey. Neither have I forgotten Jim, the horse-hero of the day, who pulled the box sleigh. In my mind I salute him, and all the other faithful, wide-eyed companions of road and furrow whose powerful, muscled haunches moved an entire society.

They ploughed and harrowed the heavy Island clay, hoisted hay into the loft on the great hayfork, turned the treadmill of the horse-power to thresh the grain and saw the firewood, and hauled produce of every kind—sacks of grain to the gristmill, cartloads of potatoes to the starch factory, and sleighloads of steaming manure all the way to the back field. They turned the capstan which was used to move a building to a new location, or to lift great forkfuls of mussel mud from the river bottom through a hole in the ice. They also went to the woods and "twitched" out logs between the stumps to the waiting bobsleigh. In the winter, after a storm, they broke the road, and in the spring when the frost went out of the mud, they pulled the heavy road scraper to level out the ruts.

When the work was done, they took you to the dance on Saturday night and to church on Sunday morning. And, when you died, they transported you to the graveyard.

Memories of horses are precious in the minds of Islanders, and while there is no great marble or granite statue commemorating their exploits, they are honoured across this province in the many chiselled sayings and stories which have survived. There is probably no aspect of the past which is recalled by the old people with such universal fondness as their great love of horses, and I don't believe I've ever talked to anyone who didn't have at least one good horse yarn. Horses were "God's own beast," was how one man expressed his feelings. Will Weeks from Fredericton once told one of his grandsons, "I was born with horses, and reared with horses, and that's how I liked it."

I was told of one farmer who kept a picture of his horse in his wallet, and another individual informed me that when he heard his father speaking about the horses of his youth he could detect in his voice "the same tone he used when he talked about his brothers and sisters." Nor were men the only ones who felt deeply about these animals. I remember clearly one woman who told me with great earnestness, "David, horses were the love of my life."

Another woman told me that, in her area, special plots of carrots were sometimes planted on the farm because they were such a treat for the horses. I also know there were many men who made a trip to the barn every night before bedtime to check in on the horses, often with a delectable of some kind in hand. Paula MacNeill from Knutford said her father "just loved his horses," and that when they were sick, "he would go to the barn and sleep with them, the way you would with a child."

A farmer who abused his horses was held in contempt by the community. There was a man from Cable Head who routinely beat his horse with a stick. Some people in the community said the animal would kill him one day, and that's exactly what happened. While working in the woods he got caught up in the sleigh and the horse dragged him to his death. In the eyes of the community he had received his just recompense. As William Blake put it, "A horse misus'd upon the road / Calls to heaven for human blood."

When cars and tractors made their appearance early in this century, it seemed offensive to some Islanders to bring in the noisy new contraptions and simply discard the reliable horse who had given so much for so long. I believe this helps to explain Islanders' strenuous

and passionate resistance to the coming of the automobile. It arose—
at least in part—out of a love of horses, and the long-established
interdependence between our two species. Life without horses was
simply inconceivable. "Why, the horse was pretty near everything,"
said one man from Mount Mellick. "It helped you work. It took you
where you wanted to go. God's soul and body! you had to have your
horses."

Many of the farm animals came and went without evoking
much sentiment, but the farm horse, who might be co-labourer with
a family for an entire generation, was different. People lamented little over the death of a cow or pig, but they did mourn their horses.
Horses were given a decent burial, and in some communities it was
considered a disgraceful, unseemly thing to sell an aged farm horse
for fox-meat.

One man told me that on their farm it was a good idea to stay
out of the way of his grieving, moody father for a few days after he had
had to put down a horse. Another farmer, from the Belfast area, expressed his remembrance of a special horse in a simple, spontaneous
eulogy: "He was a good horse. We had him until after my brother was
killed overseas. And we did away with him on the farm, and buried
him on the farm. Hired a man to do it."

Mike Byrne from the Byrne Road reflected, "There was a pride
taken in horses that was comparable to the work done by a man—or
even the family name." You can see this in some of the early farm
photographs. When a travelling "picture man," or a camera-toting
relative home from the States, would invite the family members into
the yard to pose in front of the house, it was routine for someone to
go get the horse for inclusion in the group. I have seen many such
pictures, and recall, in particular, one where the identifying names
were written underneath: Jack, Tilley, Elizabeth, June, Charles, and
Fran. You would have to see the picture to know that June was the
horse.

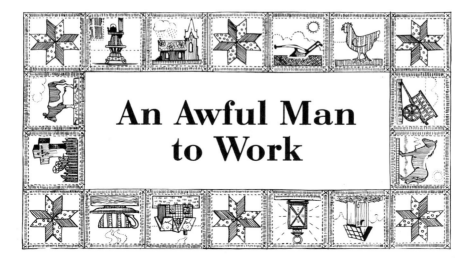

An Awful Man to Work

He watched me all day. I was working in the woods with a friend and his seventy-five-year-old father and sensed the older man silently measuring me against his own deeply ingrained standard which equated character with hard work. I could feel it every minute, with every swing of the axe, and was pleased and relieved to learn that he afterward remarked to his son, "That Weale is a pretty good man in the woods." It fell a little short of being "a great man in the woods," but I felt I had passed the test. They were all like that, men and women alike. You were judged by your capacity for labour and there was no higher compliment in that society than to be known as a good worker. When a young woman was ready to take a husband, or a young man a bride, by far the most important consideration was whether or not the prospective spouse was a good worker.

It was like an unwritten eleventh commandment, "Thou shalt work hard," and was supported by a popular proverb which reminded everyone, "The devil finds work for idle hands." A person's capacity for work was more than a question of lifestyle or personal aptitude. It was an issue of morality and the key to survival. Hard work was inherently good or virtuous, and indolence a terrible vice and a reproach on your entire family. A woman from Covehead captured this perfectly when she said, "The thing I deplore nowadays is that it is no longer a disgrace not to work."

The moral implications of work in that society are also revealed in the story of a farmer from the South Shore area who hired a boy of sixteen or seventeen who had run afoul of the law and spent some time in jail. The man realized that there would be some who would look askance at what he had done, but said in his defence that he "wanted to give the boy a chance to clear his name through hard work." Another individual who grew up in Meadowbank said his father believed in a kind of inviolable law that "if you did your work, things would work out all right for you." Yet another aged Islander confided to one of my students that, in her opinion, "Hard work and faith made everything work out."

The idea of leisure time, now a common and perfectly acceptable concept, was virtually unknown in that farming society. You might rest when you were tired, but the notion that there could be hours in the day, or days in the week, which were actually set aside for the enjoyment of leisure was unheard of, and would have sounded scandalous. One woman related that her grandfather was "an awful man to work," and a "driver" when it came to his children. She said her father growing up on the farm never knew what it was to have any "guilt-free spare time." It helps explain why the major social activity of that era, the frolic or bee, was an occasion when a little merry-making was justified by combining it with a long day of hard work.

Hazel Robinson from North Tryon shared with me a saying from that part of the Island which captures perfectly the compulsion to work. On a Monday morning it apparently was not uncommon to hear someone say, "The day after tomorrow will be the middle of the week and no work done yet."

The dogma of work was an essential creed in that farming community, but one which could weigh very heavily on the spirits of the young. Many a young man was driven off the farm by a father whose obsessiveness about work became intolerable. The farmers passed on the farms to their sons, and some of them, the wise ones, were also able to pass on a joy in the task. In many instances, however, the children received from their grim, overworked fathers a sense of oppression and resignation. I am reminded of a story told me by Reg MacEwen from York Point. He recalled a man from the North River area who was so driven by his work ethic, "He'd have his young fellows out shovelling snow off the fields in the spring, you know around the woods, so he could get it harrowed earlier. He was an awful man for that kind of thing."

80

Many of the old-timers were "awful men" in that way. An old man from Point Prim who escaped the farm for a job as a federal civil servant told me, "Oh, Father was a good man all right, and an awful man to work, but he was too hard, too hard!" Another man, asked about his childhood, responded angrily, "Childhood? What childhood? I never had a childhood. All I ever did was work." A woman from the same generation was asked to name her childhood playthings. "The broom, the mop, and the dish cloth," she quipped ironically.

Childhood, from a very early age, was an apprenticeship in farm work. You could be gathering eggs by age six, filling the woodbox by age seven, milking two cows every morning and evening by age eight, baking bread by age nine, or ploughing with two horses by age ten. Bannerman Webb from Trout River put it this way: "We were brought up to work, you know. That's all we ever knew." Some individuals recall this with gratitude, and are quick to attribute their success in life to the work habits they learned on the farm. In others, the memory of hard work is mixed with resentment and pain. I recall a man of my own generation who told me, with a catch in his voice, that in all his years growing up on the farm he never could please his father. There was sadness and a bit of anger left in him when he said, "I didn't realize until I was sixteen and hired on at another farm that I was actually a pretty good worker." Another man said he remembered only too well the "early morning rows" between himself and his father, and the "thundering across the stalls" at milking time. He said, "The stupid, clumsy animals would get punched in the ribs and kick the milk bucket," and that, in those moments, "dreams of Boston became desperate plans."

In that rural regime there were no short-cuts to success, no substitutes for hard work. You either worked hard or you sank into poverty and disgrace. The connection between physical labour and well-being was so clear and direct that working hard became for many the source of their deepest pleasure and the surest measure of their sense of self-esteem. One of my former students, after interviewing a number of senior Islanders on the topic of work, came to the conclusion, "They only really felt alive when they were working." It was an astute observation. The ability to put in a good day's work was the principal source of satisfaction in that culture, and a man from Nine Mile Creek, though admitting that he had "worked like a slave," was quick to add: "But I enjoyed it, and I don't think anybody that don't work can enjoy living."

In the diary of Barbara MacFarlane Campbell from Cape Traverse I discovered a succinct but eloquent summation of this attitude toward work. On Sunday, October 14, 1923, she penned this brief entry: "Altogether a lovely week, got a lot of work done."

Stuck Home

Sad, sad the hearts of those who leave home for some faraway destination; yet mixed with the sadness is excitement, and the anticipation of a new adventure. Sad, even more sad, are the hearts of those who stay, for mixed with their sadness is the pain of being left, and a gnawing dissatisfaction with the old familiar surroundings, now diminished by the absence of a son, daughter, lover, or friend. And they feel in their hearts how better to leave than be left.

In the late eighteenth and early nineteenth centuries, Prince Edward Island was a popular destination. Tens of thousands of refugees from the British Isles flooded into the Island for a fresh start. In the late nineteenth and early twentieth centuries that changed. Tens of thousands of young Islanders, dissatisfied with their prospects here, packed their bags and headed off to greener pastures: some to California, some to Colorado, some to western Canada, but most in a massive exodus to "the Boston States." The Island had ceased to be a destination. It had become instead a place of evacuation—a place to leave. It was no longer an island of welcome, but had become an Island of good-byes.

At first it was just a trickle. It was not long, however, before the trickle became a stream, the stream a tide, and the tide a flood. In 1891 the population of Prince Edward Island was 109,000. By 1931, despite the high birth rate, that number had plummeted to 88,000.

The grandchildren of pioneers who had arrived by the boatload were now leaving by the trainload. So many people were emigrating during these years that leaving home became a routine pattern of behaviour.

It was quite impossible for any young man or woman to grow up without asking the question, "Shall I go?" Indeed, I am certain that for most the attitude from an early age was not so much, "Shall I go?" but rather, "When shall I go?" By the time you were fourteen or fifteen, Boston began to act as a powerful magnet. Going to the States became a rite of passage into adulthood. One woman from Montague put it this way: "Going to Boston was the thing to do. Everyone was going up, or else they were already up there." And a man from Kelly's Cross had this recollection: "I was stuck home. My oldest brother came home on holidays, and I coaxed and coaxed to go back with him."

I am intrigued by the term "stuck home," which I have heard frequently. I believe it suggests poignantly the feelings of those many Islanders who wanted to get away, but who, for reasons beyond their control, were unable to leave; those who were bound and immobilized by family obligation, like shingles nailed and overlapped on the side of the barn. It became for some a source of lifelong disappointment and regret. One woman said, "I couldn't go away because my mother died when I was thirteen and I had to stay home to look after my younger brothers and sisters." Her husband's comments were remarkably similar. "My father," he reflected, "wasn't well enough, so I was needed to farm the old homestead in Valleyfield East. I couldn't leave it and go off to Boston after my father and grandfather had worked night and day to make the farm what it was."

In all of this it is possible to detect what might be termed an "outmigration trauma." It is the trauma of being left behind or, quite literally, of missing the boat. With so many of their contemporaries leaving for greener pastures, it was easy for the stay-at-homes to feel aggrieved and resentful, to think themselves deprived, and to regard the Island as a place of entrapment and missed opportunity. Further, it didn't help one bit when relatives from the States returned every summer in shiny maroon cars, dressed in fancy city fashions; or when the "Boston-box" arrived at Christmas filled with presents and hand-me-downs.

In order to cope with the insecurity and self-doubt created by outmigration, those left behind often resorted to two main types of rationalization. First, it was comforting to believe the departed

Islanders would discover, sooner or later, that the grass was not greener on the other side of the Strait and that they would, at the first opportunity, return home and reaffirm their commitment to the Island as the best place after all. Even today it is considered by some a vindication of sorts when long-departed Islanders come home to die or have their bodies sent home for interment—expressing posthumously that this was, after all, the favoured spot.

It was also psychologically helpful for the stay-at-homes to believe that the departing Islanders were not really deserting their home province but were going forth into the world as ambassadors of Islandness, spreading their innate goodness and common sense wherever they went. How often I have heard the brag that we have been a major exporter of brains. Just a few years ago one Island man compiled a massive collection of material on "successful Islanders abroad." I doubt, somehow, that he plans a sequel, "failed Islanders abroad," though I suppose there might be some comfort in that as well.

A thinly disguised anxiety about the merits of this province is revealed when Islanders begin to rhapsodize fulsomely about our "way of life," or when a visitor is asked, disingenuously, "Well now, what do you think of the Island?" The need for reassurance is sometimes painfully evident.

In a popular local radio commercial for cheese products there are two old codgers, Angus and Alex, who banter back and forth as a lead-in to their sales pitch. In one of them Angus says, "Oh Alex, there is no place like Prince Edward Island!" Alex then replies, "Yes Angus, you can go wherever you want but you'll never find a better spot than this." The dialogue makes me wince. You have to wonder, first of all, whether either Angus or Alex have ever been off the Island. It also seems to me the commercial is a clever exploitation, not of Islanders' pride, but of our ambivalence about whether or not this is, indeed, the "best place in the world." And, as I see it, one of the main reasons for that ambivalence is the departure over the years of so many to seek their fame and fortune elsewhere, leaving the rest of us "stuck home."

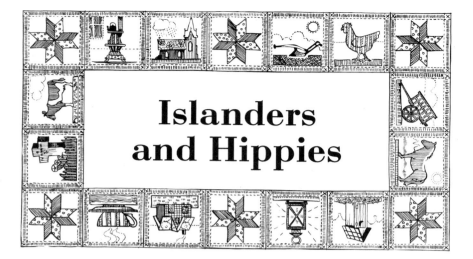

Islanders
and Hippies

For many Islanders, there was something oddly reassuring about the hippies, that motley collection of youthful refugees from middle-class America who arrived in this province in the late 1960s and early 1970s. Whether they were fleeing the draft, the authority of their parents, or the rectangular boredom of suburban existence, many of them received a surprisingly warm welcome in the rural, backroad communities of Prince Edward Island. In a province notorious for its deep-dish conservatism, the outrageously nonconformist "flower children" discovered a natural sympathy for many of their countercultural aspirations. It seemed like home.

A friend who arrived in the early 1970s and bought an abandoned farmhouse in Milltown Cross for five hundred dollars told me that initially he and his companions were "a real curiosity item." The long-time local residents weren't sure what to make of their long hair, their beads, their Taoism, and their unconventional sexual attitudes. "It was a real shock at first," he explained, "and I'm sure they thought we were crazy. But when they found out we were just trying to be ourselves, and to survive, many of them got over their astonishment. Some of them became good friends and couldn't do enough for us."

I had heard much the same story from others and was, quite frankly, surprised and not a little perplexed to learn of the support extended by many rural Islanders to these deviants from mainline

North American society. Islanders, after all, were supposed to be inveterately hostile to change of any kind; yet, here they were, extending the hand of neighbourly assistance to individuals who seemed—at least on the surface—as different as any group of people could be.

But that initial analysis left out a great deal. I now see that, within the context of traditional Island society, the hippies were in many regards an entirely conservative group. It took a while, but rural Islanders and hippies eventually discovered many basic common attitudes.

When the hippies arrived, the Island was in the throes of a social and economic revolution which had been building in momentum over the preceding decades. It was a time of letting go of a number of cherished institutions and many Islanders were deeply traumatized by the process. The province had recently embarked on a controversial "Fifteen Year Comprehensive Development Plan," and virtually every aspect of provincial life was being measured against the planning dogmas of centralization, consolidation, and modernization. The Land Development Corporation was buying up abandoned farms and the Department of Education was proceeding with its plan to close down all the little one-room schools. The apostles of change were promising a better, more rational future, but it seemed to many that the very nature of Island society was being compromised. The debate was intense and resistance widespread.

That's when the hippies got here, and though they seemed unlikely allies, most of them identified instinctively with the resistance movement. Many Islanders, they discovered, didn't like modernity any more than they did. With their "back to the land" philosophy and their idealization of rural self-sufficiency, they soon discovered a fundamental kinship with many rural folk. Disgruntled Islanders and displaced hippies discovered, to their mutual surprise, that when they got beneath their obvious external differences they were cultural soul mates—fellow champions of a disappearing way of life.

The hippies, like many rural Islanders, preferred the kind of society which existed here before "the break." They might have been naive and wildly romantic, but they possessed, nonetheless, a natural affinity for many of the customs and folkways which had been at the heart of the mixed farming economy. They longed for community, loved storytelling and old-time music, burned wood instead of oil, preferred midwives to professional obstetricians, pursued many traditional crafts, bartered when they could instead of buying, and, most importantly, desired the primal experience of working with their own hands to provide basic needs. But they were babes in the woods. Hapless and inexperienced, they often turned for advice to the long-time residents of their adopted communities. For those consulted it was affirming—even flattering. In the midst of a period when society seemed increasingly to spurn the wisdom and skills of the countryside, here were individuals who appeared genuinely appreciative of the old ways. You could overlook the drugs, the braless bosoms—even a curious affinity for goats and granola—in people like that.

A former hippie (if there is such a thing) told me recently that one of his most vivid memories of coming to the Island was travelling down the road in his beat-up van listening to Valdy on the radio singing his hit song, "Going to the Country." At a time when droves of Island young people were heading for the city, these winsome, urban-bred youngsters in bell-bottomed jeans and peasant blouses were coming to make one last gallant stand for the dignity and independence of living off the land. It seemed humourous, even absurd, yet many Islanders were secretly pleased by their coming.

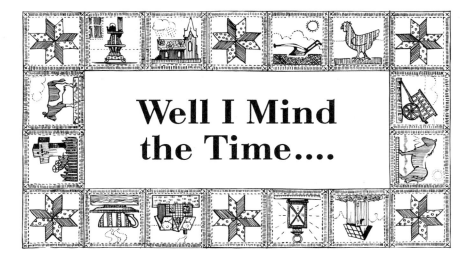

Well I Mind the Time....

I remember all the talking—especially in the evenings. The conversations had a savoury, unhurried aspect, as though there was time to speak of things both small and great, and time to listen. It seems to me there was in those conversations a quality of dialogue and sociability which has now largely disappeared from our speaking.

If the culture which existed on this Island before "the break" was clearly richer than ours in any single way, it was in the richness of its conversation. Talking and storytelling were at the very heart of that society—an oral weaving of shared experience into the fabric of intelligence and community. As surely as eggs were preserved in salt, herring in pickle, pork in its own fat, and berries in sugar, the heart and soul of the community were preserved and faithfully passed on in story.

How I loved those wonderful, finely textured stories. And they were always telling them. Down at the forge, around a quilting frame, over the fence, beside the stove in the local store, or around the kitchen table, they were forever telling stories, and each would draw the next, like tissues out of a box. With a slight shifting of position in the chair, a clearing of the throat, and the introductory phrase, "Well I mind the time...."—another story would begin.

Most everyone got in on the telling, but the best of the raconteurs were truly artists, and their storytelling a skilled performance. They told a story the way a fiddler played a tune. Timing, cadence, gestures, mimicry, and the premeditated pause were all expertly blended together into a fine art form. It was also a matter of prestige for the storyteller to be able to remember exact dates, figures, and other details associated with his repertoire. And it was a practiced art. Stories were hard-polished and refined by frequent telling until every word was exactly right, a precious stone in its proper setting.

I recall Clarence Nicolle from Murray River and one story he told about a boating mishap off Pictou Island. The telling must have lasted twenty minutes, but once Clarence began you were caught, and he played you like a fish on a line. One young man from New Argyle whose grandfather stayed at his house told me that he would sometimes hear the old man, alone in his room with the door closed, telling his stories over and over. He reasoned that his grandfather was attempting to improve his telling; but also that he said them out loud to himself just for the sheer joy of hearing them. That surely must be the ultimate test of the good storyteller, when he is able to entertain himself with his own stories.

They were consummate entertainers, with an appreciative local audience, but there was much more to the storytelling than the amusement of neighbours on a long winter's evening. It would not be too great an exaggeration to say it was the storytellers who created the community. By arranging into storied patterns the disparate strands of communal experience, they held up pictures for the community in which it was able to identify and recognize itself. Out of the chaos and incoherence of mingling human energies, definition was obtained.

The wisdom of storytelling is a wonderfully subtle wisdom, for it is the wisdom of interrelatedness. It deals with the intricate, complex web of human actions and attitudes, and is therefore closely connected to the actual processes of daily life, rather than being a lesson which is abstracted from life and frozen into a principle. The stories provided the means for expressing and experiencing the entire range of human emotion. Anger, affection, envy, contempt, admiration—they were all there; and, because of this mirroring of the passion of the community, there was an intimacy experienced at the level of the community—a sense of knowing and being known. Because the individual's life was a thread woven into the fabric of the story, there was a powerful experience of self-realization and, simultaneously, of belonging to something greater than yourself.

It was a sad and inauspicious moment that first evening the local storyteller went across the field to the neighbour's house for a visit only to discover that he had been displaced by the radio, for the beginning of the end of storytelling was the beginning of the end of the Island. There were stories on the radio all right, but they weren't our stories, and a community or nation without its own storytellers is a society created and defined by outsiders; a community without integrity; one alienated from its own genius.

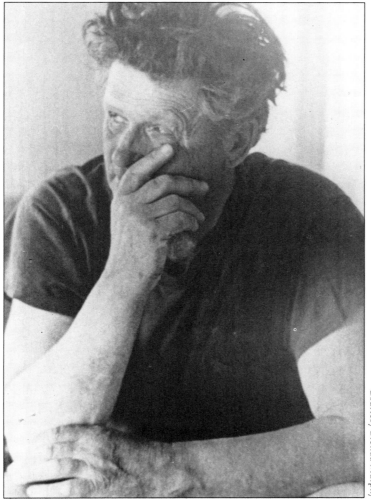

Courtesy Brenda Murphy

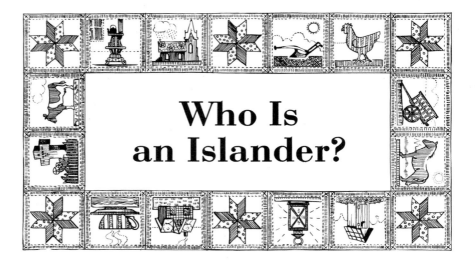

Who Is
an Islander?

I had just finished giving an address and was chatting with someone who had come forward to ask a question. Off to the side,
within earshot, two older women were waiting for the room to
clear. They were talking about the lecture and I overheard one of
them remark to her friend, "But he's not an Islander, is he?" Without
a moment's hesitation, the other woman responded, "No dear, he's
not, but he's lived here all his life."

Who is an Islander? Someone whose people have been here
since the Napoleonic Wars? Someone conceived above the high
water mark? Someone who says "slippy" instead of slippery, and
"pataduh" instead of potato? Like most Islanders, I've participated
in that discussion many times, often seriously, more often whimsi-
cally. But something happened a couple of years ago which settled it
for me.

I was driving one day with my ten-year-old son along the shore
to a late-afternoon ball game in Rustico. He sat quietly in his seat,
just looking out the window at the passing landscape and seascape.
I glanced his way several times, but he didn't even notice. He was
absorbed in his looking. Then it occurred to me what he was doing.
He was taking in the landscape. He was, if you will, ingesting the
Island.

That is usually what happens when you live on the Island for
long, and is always what happens when you live here as a child. You

take it inside—deep inside. First you inhabit the Island, then the Island inhabits you, and you live it from the inside out. Islandness becomes a part of your being, as deep as marrow and as unself-conscious as body language. You begin with an Island name, but in the end you have Island blood.

Wherever you look in the world you discover peoples whose lives have been shaped by their habitat. There are mountain people, valley people, and people of the prairie; polar people, coastal people, and people of the forest. In each case the nature of the society, its mythology, its imagination, its very spirit, has been sculpted and coloured by its natural environment. It is that way here. The people who live in this province—most of us at least—are island people, and when we say, "We are Islanders," it is simply the acknowledgement that we have taken the Island inside, and that we have an island psyche, an island soul.

I have concluded that the quintessential uniqueness of an island is its geographic distinctiveness. It may sound like a truism, but I believe that's the heart of the matter. "An island," as I was taught in grade three, "is a body of land completely surrounded by water," or, as a friend from Cape Breton recently expressed it, "An island is geographically perfect." A mandala, if you will.

Lord Tweedsmuir, Governor General of Canada, made the following remarks in a speech delivered in Charlottetown in 1939. "What is it," he asked, "that gives an island its special charm...? I think the main reason is that an Island has clear physical limits, and the mind is able to grasp it and make a picture of it as whole." Once again it is noteworthy that Tweedsmuir was speaking, not just of a topographical shoreline but also, in the words of a friend, of the "psychological shoreline" which has been internalized in the consciousness of Islanders and informs every aspect of life in this province. This deep truth about ourselves is also expressed simply and eloquently in Milton Acorn's poem, "The Island":

Since I'm Island-born home's as precise
as if a mumbly old carpenter,
shoulder-straps crossed wrong,
laid it out,
refigured to the last three-eighths of shingle.

And so, my son, I'm happy you were gazing out the window that day as we passed by cropped fields, carved woodlots, and errant estuaries fingering in from the Gulf. I'm happy for the great hunched heron you noticed in the marsh by the bridge, and the terns, sky-wheeling over guardian dunes and terraced sandstone ledges. I'm glad you took it all in; glad for your meditation on this Island place where you will always belong and which, wherever you go, will always be a part of you.

Kitchen Table
Surgery

The kitchen was the heart of the farm, and at the centre of the kitchen was the table. In the daily round of chores and activities, everything flowed out from and then back to that ritual location. At mealtimes, and many other times, it was the tribal gathering spot for family members and their friends.

Most of what occurred there was pleasant. In some homes the wide, oilcloth-covered table was a family altar as mother and children knelt at their chairs while an earnest Presbyterian father laboured through one of the Psalms and led in morning prayer. In Roman Catholic homes it was often the scene where family members—at least some of them—day-dreamed through the Rosary. In the evening it was a study desk. Children pulled up close to a single coal-oil lamp to memorize long poems or calculate long sums in an unlined scribbler with coarse, gray paper inside and the picture of a Mountie on the cover. In the winter, during long dark evenings from December to March, it was a games table: a place for checkers and cards and the slide and click of crokinole pieces.

It was also a work table. Harness might be mended there, or Sunday clothes ironed, or sooty lamp chimneys cleaned, or eggs washed for market, or a leather clapper for the broken pump improvised out of an old boot tongue.

These were all part of the routine ebb and flow of country living. But life, unfortunately, was not always routine. There were stark times of sickness and tragedy; desperate, frozen moments in the life of the family when the doctor would arrive with his small bag of surgical instruments. It was then, out of dire necessity, that the kitchen table became an operating table.

Tonsillectomies, mastoidectomies, the suturing of wounds, and the setting of bones were commonplace. But the kitchen was also the scene of other, more major operations. Appendectomies, mastectomies, amputations, and the removal of tumours—these also were performed on the kitchen table.

A man from Montague recalled the time in 1920 that his mother and one of his brothers both ended up with pus in their lungs from a bad case of pneumonia. They were doing so poorly that Doctor Preston MacIntyre was called in. He arrived by sleigh with a bottle of ether and his little bag of tools. Then, right there on the kitchen table, he took a piece of rib out of each of them, drained off the pus, spread a little sulphur, sewed them back up, and put them back to bed. They both recovered. When I expressed my amazement at this to Jean Macdonald of Brudenell, a nurse who sometimes worked with Doctor MacIntyre, she just laughed and said, "Oh, that was nothing out of the ordinary. It was all in a day's work for the Doctor back then."

It was often necessary for a doctor to improvise under those makeshift circumstances. Doctor MacIntyre told me a story about the time he was called to a place where the woman was suffering from severe postpartum hemorrhaging. She had lost so much blood there was no pulse. "There was no intravenous at that time," he explained, "but I got an old enema bag. The water from the pump was all riley and sandy. I had to strain it three times, and it was still red. But I boiled that and made a saline solution, one teaspoon of salt to one pint of water." Then, in his characteristically cryptic style he added, "That pulled her through."

He said that on another occasion he was in a home where the guttering light from a single lamp was so dim he couldn't see what he was doing. He put down his scalpel, went outside, pulled his car up to the kitchen window, and shone his headlights on the prostrate patient. He then went back in and finished the job.

Missing
Fingers

When I was a child, and still wondering about all those things that children quietly observe, I was intrigued by the hands of the farmers in my community. They were not especially big men, but many of them had very large hands with thick powerful fingers and the devil's own grip. Of special, morbid fascination were all the hands with missing fingers and thumbs.

You'd notice it when they would roll a cigarette or when they'd be fumbling for money in their wallets, or "purses" as they were then called. You might also notice when they would be buttering a slice of bread, or putting a cup of tea to their lips. Most of them just had a small piece or two missing; perhaps just a tip, or a finger cut back to the second knuckle because the doctor needed skin enough to sew up. One man had lost a thumb, and I can still recall how awkwardly he would grasp at things between his fingers and the palm of his hand.

Most interesting was the man who played the guitar at house parties. His chording hand was intact, but his strumming hand had been badly chewed up. The odd thing was that he had lost entirely both his index finger and his little finger, and as I watched him play I would try to imagine what possible accident could have taken those two fingers and left the other two untouched.

Fingers could be bitten off, or frozen off, and one man I know, a railwayman, got his hand jammed in the coupling between two railway cars. But, as anyone might guess, the most common cause of finger loss was either from accidents around machinery, or the chopping and sawing of wood. Usually it was the result of simple inattention or carelessness—but not always. Two brothers, John and Gerald, were chopping wood together. John, apparently in a whimsical mood, said to Gerald, "Put your finger on the block there and I'll chop it off for you." Gerald, apparently in the same mood, laid his finger on the block as directed, fully expecting his brother to halt the downward trajectory of the axe before it reached its intended destination. John, on the other hand, brought down the axe fully expecting his brother to pull back. But they were both wrong, and the result was one more hand with one less finger.

Another man cut off the end of his finger at the chopping block and rushed to the doctor in the village, who cleaned the stump and sewed it up. As he was leaving the doctor said, "It was a clean cut, Johnnie. If you had brought in the tip we might have been able to save it."

"I thought of that," responded the patient in disgust, "but before I could get it one of the goddamn chickens made off with it."

The Forge

Come along with me, down the road to the corner, down to the ringing forge. Here, where the nut-coal fire glows, and the anvil sings, I will show you a place where new, strong things are made, and old, broken things mended.

Come meet a man, all grime and grease and runneled with sweat; a tough, indomitable, cursing man who teases and tortures the iron to the shape of his intent. With hammer and heat he makes custom-fitted shoes for the horses, anchors for fishermen, ploughs for farmers, mudforks for the muddiggers, crosses for the dead, and wheels for the living. He'll even pull your teeth if you ask him.

This forge is more than a workplace. It is also a place for men to congregate, a fraternity hall of fellowship and escape. There is laughter here, and gossip, and spitting, and conversation which fills in the spaces between the hammer's pounding like water running between rocks.

What great fascination and male-magic there is in this small, sooty building with its bellows lung and strong anvil pulse. And sometimes the children can be seen around the outer edge of things, in the gallery seats. Here are the best stories they will ever hear; the best theatre they will ever see.

He can make almost anything, this blacksmith, for he is part artisan and part sorcerer. With his split leather apron he stands bent beside the ancient fire, and, like his father and grandfather before him, he fashions the instruments of labour and conquest. Amid a shower of sparks he draws from the mute metal its hidden service and beauty. The rhythmic rising and falling of his great hammer is the percussion beat of human perseverance, counterpoint to harsh survival, pounding back through centuries to days of stone.

Courtesy Merrill Weale

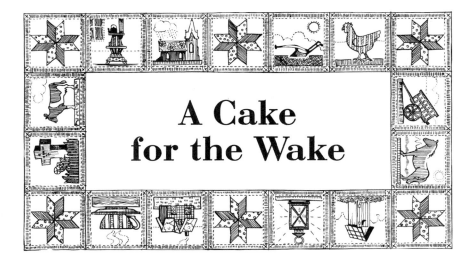

A Cake
for the Wake

D id you ever notice there are some people who can scarcely bring themselves to say the words "dead" or "died"? None of their acquaintances ever actually die, they just "pass away." My friend John Cousins told one once about a boy—I think his name was William—who had gone to Nova Scotia to work in the woods. While there, he became sick and died quite unexpectedly. The woman who ran the boarding house where he was staying was one of those people who found it difficult to come right out and speak of such matters. She sent a letter with the bad news to the family, in which she referred mysteriously to "William's great change."

Perhaps it was the polarized Christian view of things, where death is often perceived as the great, dark opposite of life, which made it so difficult to be comfortable with the mystery of dying. It seemed so unnatural, so sinister. Perhaps that is also why there was a great deal of death humour, for surely it is the gift of humour that allows us to laugh in the presence of those things which make us most anxious and afraid. I suppose you might even say that death humour, far from being irreverent, was a kind of backhanded tribute to the seriousness of the subject. Whatever the reasons, Islanders told many humourous stories around the topic of death. I suspect it was their way, orally, of dancing at the wake.

The humour tended to be camouflaged, sardonic, and understated, rather like the people themselves. In a province where emotional candour and forthrightness were not encouraged, it was often the skilful probe of wry wit which touched the submerged passion, allowing for a momentary breaking forth, in laughter, of concealed opinion.

One story tells of a funeral service being held at the little white Presbyterian church in Canoe Cove. It was a cold, nasty day and the mourners were standing around the open grave, shoulders hunched against the sharp wind, waiting for the committal. One old man from the community, shrunken and frail, stood there shivering. Beside him was a younger man who couldn't resist the temptation of the moment. "Fred," he said, "the look of you today, I don't think it worth your while going home."

In another story, an old man, frail and dying, was lying in the little room off the kitchen, very near his end. His wife was busy baking, and the aroma of her cooking filled the house. It roused him a bit.

"Marion," he called out feebly, "what are you baking? Is it dark fruit cake?"

"Yes," she replied, "it is."

"Oh!" he said, "my favourite. Could I have a piece when it is finished?"

"No dear," she responded curtly, "it's for the wake."

There is obviously more to that story—much more—than the drama of dying. The delicate matter of marital relations, no less a source of anxiety than death itself, is also being treated with the deft therapy of folk humour.

It is the same in this next story about an old woman who lay dying. She thought it might be her last night on earth so she asked her husband to sit up with her until the end. He agreed and remained by the bedside through the long night vigil. But she didn't die, and the next night made the same request. "No, no, Mary," he scolded. "You fooled me last night. I'll not let you fool me again tonight."

There is a wide range of human difficulties and predicaments which individuals attempt to address with humour. In the next story it is once again the occasion of death, with its power to shake out the truth, which provided precisely the right moment for the bringing forth of a sentiment obviously longing for expression. Further, it

Courtesy Lillie Watts

seems likely that in the telling and retelling of this story, the entire community discovered an ingenious way of getting even.

In a Scottish district about twenty miles east of Charlottetown lived an old codger named Thornton, a man with a very long beard. Thornton was not well-liked, for apparently he had the annoying habit of taking things that didn't belong to him. If someone left a stack of lumber in the yard, and in the morning there were several pieces missing, it was generally assumed that Thornton had passed by. But, as was so often the case in those rural communities, the behaviour, though disliked, was tolerated. As long as your deviance didn't become too extreme, the neighbours would simply put up with it, and deal with the frustration in their stories.

When Thornton died, the funeral was held from his home. It was a bitterly cold winter day and there was a big fire blazing. Most of Thornton's neighbours were in attendance and the house was crowded. One woman, wearing fur, came in late and had to sit in a chair by the red-hot stove. When everyone was asked to stand for the final prayer, her coat brushed against the stove and the pungent smell of singed hair filled the room. Seizing the moment, one irreverent fellow leaned over to the man next to him and whispered, "Old Thornton must have landed. I can smell his whiskers burning."

Sometimes the death humour was intentional. Other times it was accidental—or at least unconscious, like the telegram sent from a Moar man in New Perth to his sister in Boston. Their mother had died, but the man didn't want the news to be all bad so he sent a message which read: "MOTHER IS DEAD ALL IS WELL."

The Christmas Concert

I t was the closest thing to a gala occasion that many rural folk would ever attend; the most important, eagerly anticipated event on the social calendar. It was the Christmas concert. The entire community would be there; everyone who could move, or be moved, packed into the one-room school house or community hall which for that night was transformed into a centre for the performing arts.

The teacher, poor thing, was production supervisor, artistic director, and stage manager, all rolled into one. For her it was quite literally a trial. Any teacher who couldn't put together a good Christmas concert just wouldn't last long. As one former teacher told me, "You had to have a good concert or woe betide you." Weeks of preparation were required, during which time ordinary lessons were almost suspended. Then, finally, when all the lines were memorized, all the costumes made, and all the spruce garlands and tissue-paper roses in place, the big night arrived.

How delightfully the scene stands out in memory. I recall the nickering of horses and jangling of sleigh-bells in the schoolyard as people arrived, and how wonderfully bright the windows were from the gas lanterns brought from homes and hung on walls. I recall the white sheets strung across the front on a piece of number nine wire, with a big, self-conscious boy at either end, and the school trustee, in his rumpled brown Sunday suit who stood up at the start and

105

awkwardly welcomed everyone. I recall the ten-cent packages of homemade fudge in little brown paper bags at intermission, and the pencil box with the sliding top which I received from the teacher who was expected to have a present for everyone. But most of all I recall the excitement of waiting for the THUMP, THUMP, THUMP, on the door. "He's here, he's here!" we would all cry out, and, with that, Santa Claus would make his grand entrance.

He didn't look at all like today's Santa Claus with his stylish costume of red and white. Santa then was quite a different, more earthy creature. He wore a heavy, knee-length fur coat, and a stocking cap, with a string of sleigh-bells around his ample waist, and a pair of new boots, just like the pair Freddie's uncle had on in church the previous Sunday. And one year, in the middle of everything, he passed right out from the heat in the hall and, I suspect, from the Christmas "shine" he had been sampling before his arrival.

Looking back as an adult, it occurs to me that there were probably many in attendance for whom the evening was an ordeal of noise and confusion. But for a seven-year-old, who didn't even know the word, it was a night of enchantment.

There was one Christmas concert I will never forget. That year Santa arrived carrying two bags over his shoulder, one filled with presents, and one which wriggled and jounced with some form of concealed life. "I've got a present here you'll have to catch," he announced, and with that he dumped out on the floor a small brown puppy which began to run through the crowd. Many hands reached out for him, mine included. He came near where I was standing, and, for a moment, it seemed possible that I might be lucky enough to grab him. But just then a farmer standing beside me—Marshall Rayner I believe—reached down and scooped him up. My disappointment was great, my hopes dashed. Then I heard the man say, "David, do you have a dog?" "No," I stammered. "Then here's something for you," he said, as he placed the frightened little creature in my arms.

It was a sublime moment, and I have the suspicion that every Christmas since then has been anticipated and silently measured against that long ago event when God appeared on earth during the Christmas concert in the form of a puppy. Walking home that night in the snow with that little dog in my arms I had some inkling of what Mary might have experienced. She could not have felt more blessed.

Suppertime

It was twilight, that last surrendering part of the day when darkness mixes in with the light, and the sharp images of landscape disappear silently into the hungering night. We were playing in Elmer Hammill's field near the ditch. Along the line fence, a family of tall spruce, their separate tops in silhouette against the pewter sky, dissolved together in shadows near the ground. It could have been yesterday, but we were children then, neither remembering nor waiting, still pagan, creatures of the dusk, happy and vital in the long grass, using up the last wash of evening brightness.

It was suppertime: the call had just come. Time to cross the road and go inside that old gabled house with wild rose bushes up close against the step and a rough storm door hooked back against the shingles until the first snow. There was wood-warmth there, yellow coal-oil lamplight against the walls, the smell of fried potatoes, and a dog on the mat. It was nothing out of the ordinary, but it seemed the safest, warmest, most pleasant and complete place that ever could be. And from that day to this I have always known exactly what a kitchen should be, and the full meaning of the word supper.

Of all the thousands of times I went through that door into the kitchen, why do I recall so vividly that one late autumn entry? Sometimes it seems my entire childhood is in that moment, and a reminder of all that has been sacrificed to the preoccupations of adult practicality. After all these years, it stands out clearly in memory like the remembered fragment of some largely forgotten dream.

The Change That Has Come Over God

In conversations with older Islanders over the past few years, I have routinely asked the question, "What is the biggest change that has taken place in your lifetime?" Some have mentioned the coming of the automobile, others the breakdown of community life, and one woman replied without hesitation, "Getting a wringer washer. That was the big thing for me."

One of the most thoughtful responses I received to my inquiry was from a man who replied, "There have been many great changes in my lifetime, but I do believe that the greatest change of all is the change that has come over God." I smiled in surprise, and he continued. "When I was a boy growin' up, God was something to be feared. Oh yes! The fear of God was drilled into us every chance they got. That's how they kept us on the straight and narrow, by puttin' the fear of hell in us."

The speaker was a Roman Catholic, but there was nothing exclusively Catholic about his comments. Virtually all the immigrants to Prince Edward Island came from European Christian stock, and, although approximately half of them were Protestant and the other half Roman Catholic, they shared a common religious heritage. While some of them brought Bibles and others beads, while some of them upheld the presbytery and others the papacy, and while some of them wouldn't bake a cake on Sunday and others wouldn't eat meat on Friday, they were all shoots off the same stem. And when they prayed, they addressed the same sombre Divinity.

Whether they were Baptists from Bedeque, Presbyterians from Pinette, or Roman Catholics from Rustico, the deity they worshipped was "the man upstairs"—a rather censorious, patriarchal figure represented in the community by austere, male authority figures dressed in black. In Sunday School or at Catechism, all were instructed in "the fear of the Lord," and spent their lives attempting to stay on the good side of His manifestly irascible nature. You might attempt to accomplish this by fasting and going to confession, or by honouring the Sabbath and reading your Bible, but in both cases the experience was one which included a great deal of trepidation and placation. As another man confided, "I can tell you right now I didn't like Him much. Who would? He seemed to disapprove of the very appetites He had put in us. Not only that, He watched all the time, every little misstep. And if you stumbled, He was right there, on the spot, to wag His big finger."

There were, to be sure, elements of the faith which helped to soften somewhat the awful scowl of the Almighty. The kind intercession of the gentle Mary; the image of Jesus, the Good Shepherd, seeking out the lost wayward lamb; or the advocacy of guardian angels or patron saints were all ingredients of devotion which made it easier to bear up under the heavy ascription of sin and judgement. But God had the last word, and He was a distant, offended potentate with a propensity to be eternally out of sorts. "I remember," said one woman, "that when it would thunder, some of the old people would say, 'Don't you know, that's the angry voice of our Lord.'"

But much has changed these past few decades. God, it seems, has lightened up. In the privacy of individual conscience, a metamorphosis has occurred, and while most Islanders still believe in God, for many it is a God with a different, more sympathetic visage. The aloof, immutable God of the creeds has cracked a smile and shed a tear, and multitudes have sighed in grateful relief. "When I was a boy," explained one elderly Islander, "I viewed God as a great big person with a stick. I believe that kind of God was put into our heads by the priests and ministers, but now I see God as an accepting person, ready to understand and forgive."

When he finished I couldn't help thinking that his words sounded like something straight out of the Gospels.

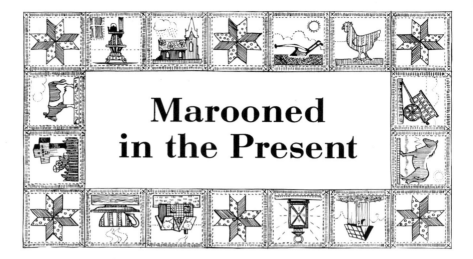

Marooned
in the Present

The people who are old today are men and women from a different time. They have outlived a civilization. The rural culture of their childhood, with roots extending far back into the distant European past, has largely disappeared, and many feel stranded on an unfamiliar and unfriendly shore where there is little demand for their skills and little respect for their wisdom. A revolution has occurred and it is easy for them to feel by times like victims of the new order of things.

The young people around them seem invariably to equate old with old-fashioned. After all, how could anyone who grew up in an age before instant coffee and credit cards, moonshots and minivans, or penicillin and psychoanalysis possibly have any useful contribution to make in this cybernetic age? An elderly woman confided to me that when she was a girl she believed old people knew everything. Now, she sighed, her grandchildren are more liable to assume that she knows nothing. It makes her feel outdated—as though she has lived too long.

The pathos of these displaced old men and women is somehow captured for me in the true story of two brothers of my acquaintance. I haven't seen either one of them for years, but when I was a boy they farmed just up the road. I was often at their places, and though they probably didn't realize it, I liked them both very much, with that secret affection that children have for kind adults, and that silent admiration boys give to strong older men.

These two raised their families side by side, with just an orchard and a lane between their houses. They dug potatoes together, got in and out of fox-farming together, fished trout together, went to church together, and grew old together. I made a sentimental journey to their farms about two years ago, but the scene was almost unrecognizable. The houses were both still there, but only the brook at the back, resplendent with yellow cowslips, touched that deep memory of long ago joy.

Donald was the first to sell the farm. He and his wife had raised more than a dozen children, but not one chose to stay there. Neil hung on a little longer, but it was the same at his place. All the children left, and, before long, he was gone too.

Now they are old, living in the city, and tragically, both are suffering from Alzheimer's disease. They never see one another; probably wouldn't recognize one another. I am told, however, that they share an unusual characteristic. When Donald looks in a mirror, he sometimes thinks it is Neil he is seeing, and speaks to him of things long ago, from a different time. Across town, in the nursing home where he is kept, Neil looks in the mirror and thinks it is Donald. He too talks of things long gone; long gone, but not forgotten.

Sound of mind or not, there are many like them in this province, displaced seniors, marooned in the present, their children and grandchildren cast adrift from the past. The dialogue of the generations has largely ceased, for they are elders without honour, and offspring without ancestry.

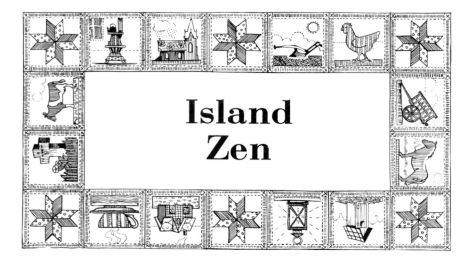

Island
Zen

Harold MacLeod, a thoughtful man, lived most of his life in Irishtown. He told me once that when he recalled the faces of neighbours he couldn't think of one that was truly sorrowful or unhappy. I never forgot that, and have often wondered about it. Is it possible that those people who worked so hard and had so little were contented?

I am, of course, aware of what is called selective memory, that capacity in people to block out what was harsh or difficult and to remember only what was pleasant. It's what makes the "good old days" so good. But the question refuses to go away. Despite the hardship, drudgery, and limited horizons of that society, was there perhaps a peace which graced the lives of its inhabitants, a peace which now eludes most of us? It's the kind of thing you could never demonstrate conclusively, but after conversations with many elderly Islanders I'm inclined to think there is something to it. I'm also inclined to believe it had something to do with meditation.

I'm not suggesting for a minute that there was any conscious or deliberate discipline of meditation. Not at all. The very word would have sounded suspiciously esoteric. What I am suggesting is that the opportunity for contemplation was built right into the order of that society: a kind of unself-conscious Island Zen which contributed greatly to emotional well-being. There were worries aplenty, but many of the mindless, monotonous, repetitious tasks provided regularly the occasion to slip underneath your cares into a still place of forgetfulness and equilibrium. Whether you were following horses, thinning turnips, hooking mats, pulling teats, picking blueberries, stacking wood, ironing shirts, grading potatoes, spinning yarn, stooking grain, or knitting mitts, there were frequent periods when physical labour could be combined with mental repose. Then, at the end of every week, there was the enforced idleness of the Sabbath. All of that might not have contributed greatly to what we call intellectual development, but my guess is that it was the source of a deeper, more fertile wisdom.

I suspect, as well, that the habitual, intimate interaction with the natural order of living things was a powerful reminder of the deep eternal movement of regeneration. Daily contact with plants and animals, and with the elemental seasonal forces of sun, wind, and weather, created a strong inviolable rhythm which underscored all activity, and modified greatly the frenetic tendencies of human compulsion. Nature is often wild, but seldom frantic.

There was a proclamation of the deep movement of creation in each season of the annual cycle, but summer was the time of mature eloquence, when nature was bright with revelation. In the profusion of summer flowering was testimony to all the great mysteries of concealed grace: praise and profession in the open face of the daisy, rapture in the celestial blue of roadside chicory, penance in a swath of purple vetch, and atonement in crimson blots of wild elderberry beneath the cruciform of a great dying spruce.

There was one custom on many farms which must have had a wonderfully restorative power. On a summer's evening, after all the inside and outside chores were finally completed, many folk would sit quietly, either on the verandah or in the sunporch, or perhaps just in the kitchen, and enjoy the stillness of the twilight. One woman referred to this as "sitting in the evening," and said it was a blessed time on their farm. In that utterly inexorable part of the day, of lengthening shadows and fading light, the quietness broken only by last birdsong, they just sat, and the serenity of the evening seeped in until it touched and mingled with the deep serenity of their own persons.

It was a time of letting go and letting be in a spirit of benediction and relaxed resignation; of being still and knowing that God, after all, is God. And sometimes, just at dusk, there would be fireflies, winking and flashing along the edge of the woods, celebrating the descending darkness, backdrop to their small shining.

Courtesy Mary Cairns

Them Times

I sat with them many evenings
around their kitchen table in High Bank.
They seemed to me an ancient folk,
like persons from a different age—
which they were.

As the conversation began to flow
I became a time traveller
for these people had first-hand knowledge
of a disappeared era.
With their stories
and talk
they beckoned me back,
back to a world they called
"them times."

Back to a time
of rising with the sun,
planting by the moon,
and living off the land.

Back to a time
of small fields and hedgerows,
quilts stretched out in frames,
barrels held together with hoops,
wheels circumscribed by iron rims,
and communities bounded by custom.

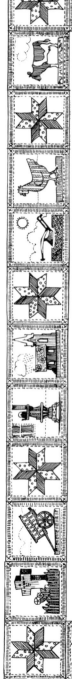

Back to a time
of water raised from a well,
mussel mud lifted from the river bottom,
soup ladled from the stock pot,
and humour extracted from predicament.

Back to a time
of banning the automobile,
prohibiting liquor,
resisting Daylight Saving Time,
and guarding against extravagance.

Back to a time
of winding the winch for water,
pumping the organ for sound,
cranking the car for power,
and rocking the cradle for peace.

Back to a time
of manners,
morals,
church every Sunday,
and a rum bottle stashed in the grain bin.

Back to a time
of egg money in a cracked cup,
savings deposited in a sock,
a shiny quarter in the baby's hand,
and large brown pennies
on dead men's eyes.

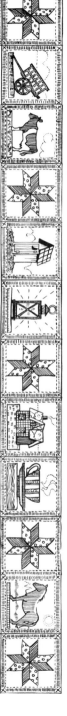

Back to a time
of old men in new cars,
and new brides in old kitchens.

Back to a time
of winters without eggs,
Lent without meat,
workers without watches,
doctors without pills,
birthdays without presents,
weddings without honeymoons,
funerals without undertakers,
bedrooms without closets,
deals without signatures,
children without shoes,
women without choices,
and men without tears.

Back to a time
of squaring fieldstone for foundations,
squaring logs for carrying beams,
squaring butter for barter,
and squaring opinion for acceptance.

Back to a time
of the spectre of debt,
the scourge of blight,
the plague of tuberculosis.
and the epidemic of guilt.

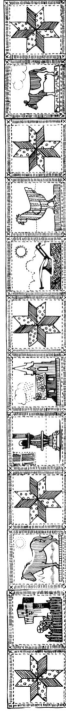

Back to a time
when a "chain" was the measure of
    your property,
a "skein" the measure of your yarn,
a "teddy" the measure of your moonshine,
a "grist" the measure of your grain,
and "industry" the measure of
    your character.

Back to a time
of kittens in the barn,
chickens on the step,
rats under the barracks,
a runt piglet behind the kitchen stove,
and a "buffalo" in the sleigh.

Back to a time
of picking stones off the land,
mustard out of the oats,
bugs off the potatoes,
and burdocks out of the fleece.

Back to a time
of home remedies:
tansy tea,
sulphur and molasses tonic,
the mustard plaster,
kerosene in a spoon,
salt herring in your socks,
and cobwebs to stop the bleeding.

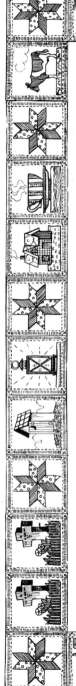

Back to a time
of separating cream from milk,
chaff from grain,
and Protestants from Catholics.

Back to a time
of free-range ducks in the yard,
and foraging visits
house to house
of the local gossip.

Back to a time
of following tradition,
following horses,
following politics,
and following in your parents' footsteps.

Back to a time
of the coming of the car,
the arrival of the tractor,
the installing of the lights,
the ringing in of the telephone,
the intrusion of the radio,
the infiltration of new ideas,
the dying out of storytelling,
and
the beginning of the end
of "them times."